BEING ADIVASI

RETHINKING INDIA
Series editors: Aakash Singh Rathore, Mridula Mukherjee,
Pushparaj Deshpande and Syeda Hameed

OTHER BOOKS IN THE SERIES
Vision for a Nation: Paths and Perspectives
(Aakash Singh Rathore and Ashis Nandy, eds)

The Minority Conundrum: Living in Majoritarian Times
(Tanweer Fazal, ed.)

Reviving Jobs: An Agenda for Growth
(Santosh Mehrotra, ed.)

We the People: Establishing Rights and Deepening Democracy
(Nikhil Dey, Aruna Roy and Rakshita Swamy, eds)

The Shudras: Vision for a New Path
(Kancha Ilaiah Shepherd and Karthik Raja Karuppusamy, eds)

Her Right to Equality: From Promise to Power
(Nisha Agrawal, ed.)

RETHINKING INDIA

BEING
ADIVASI

EXISTENCE,
ENTITLEMENTS,
EXCLUSION

Edited by
ABHAY FLAVIAN XAXA
G.N. DEVY

VINTAGE
An imprint of Penguin Random House

VINTAGE

USA | Canada | UK | Ireland | Australia
New Zealand | India | South Africa | China

Vintage is part of the Penguin Random House group of companies
whose addresses can be found at global.penguinrandomhouse.com

Published by Penguin Random House India Pvt. Ltd
4th Floor, Capital Tower 1, MG Road,
Gurugram 122 002, Haryana, India

Penguin
Random House
India

First published in Vintage by Penguin Random House India 2021

Typeset in Bembo Std by Manipal Technologies Limited, Manipal
Printed at Replika Press Pvt. Ltd, India

www.penguin.co.in

Contents

I Am Not Your Data

I am not your data, nor am I your vote bank,
I am not your project or any exotic museum object,
I am not the soul waiting to be harvested,
nor am I the lab where your theories are tested,
I am not your cannon fodder or the invisible worker,
or your entertainment at India Habitat Centre,
I am not your field, your crowd, your history,
your help, your guilt, medallions of your victory,
I refuse, reject, resist your labels,
your judgments, documents, definitions,
your models, leaders and patrons,
because they deny me my existence, my vision, my space,
your words, maps, figures, indicators,
they all create illusions and put you on a pedestal,
from where you look down upon me.
So I draw my own picture, and invent my own grammar,
I make my own tools to fight my own battle,
For me, my people, my world and my Adivasi self!

—Abhay Flavian Xaxa*

---

* This poem by Abhay Flavian Xaxa was earlier published by Round Table India.

Series Editors' Note

Psychologists tell us that the only true enemies we have are the faces looking back at us in the mirror. Today, we in India need to take a long, hard look at ourselves in the mirror. With either actual or looming crises in every branch of government, at every level, be it central, state or local; with nearly every institution failing; with unemployment at historically high rates; with an ecosystem ready to implode; with a healthcare system in a shambles; with an education system on the brink of collapse; with gender, caste and class inequities unabating; with civil society increasingly characterized by exclusion, intolerance and violence; with our own minorities living in fear; our hundreds of millions of fellow citizens in penury; and with few prospects for the innumerable youth of this nation in the face of all these increasingly intractable problems, the reflection is not sightly. Our true enemies are not external to us, not Pakistani terrorists or Bangladeshi migrants, but our own selves: our own lack of imagination, communication, cooperation and dedication towards achieving the India of our destiny and dreams.

Our Constitution, as the preamble so eloquently attests, was founded upon the fundamental values of the dignity of the individual and the unity of the nation, envisioned in relation to a radically egalitarian justice. These bedrock ideas, though perhaps especially pioneered by the likes of Jawaharlal Nehru, B.R. Ambedkar, M.K. Gandhi, Maulana Azad, Sardar Patel, Sarojini Naidu, Jagjivan Ram, R. Amrit Kaur, Ram Manohar Lohia and others, had emerged as a broad consensus among the many founders of this nation, cutting across divergent social and political ideologies. Giving shape to that vision, the architects of modern India strived to ensure that each one of us is accorded equal opportunities to live with dignity and security, has equitable access to a better life, and is an equal partner in this nation's growth.

Yet, today we find these most basic constitutional principles under attack. Nearly all the public institutions that were originally created in order to fight against dominance and subservience are in the process of subversion, creating new hierarchies instead of dismantling them, generating inequities instead of ameliorating them. Government policy merely pays lip service to egalitarian considerations, while the actual administration of 'justice' and implementation of laws are in fact perpetuating precisely the opposite: illegality, criminality, corruption, bias, nepotism and injustice of every conceivable stripe. And the rapid rise of social intolerance and manifold exclusions (along the lines of gender, caste, religion, etc.) effectively whittle down and even sabotage an inclusive conception of citizenship, polity and nation.

In spite of these and all the other unmentioned but equally serious challenges posed at this moment, there are in fact new sites for sociopolitical assertion re-emerging. There are new calls arising for the reinstatement of the letter and spirit of our Constitution, not just normatively (where we battle things out ideologically) but also practically (the battle at the level of policy articulation and implementation). These calls are not simply partisan, nor are they exclusionary or zero-sum. They witness the wide participation of youth, women, the historically disadvantaged in the process of finding a new voice, minorities, members of majority communities, and progressive individuals all joining hands in solidarity.

We at the Samruddha Bharat Foundation proudly count ourselves among them. The Foundation's very raison d'être has been to take serious cognizance of India's present and future challenges, and to rise to them. Over the past two years, we have constituted numerous working groups to critically rethink social, economic and political paradigms to encourage a transformative spirit in India's polity. Over 400 of India's foremost academics, activists, professionals and policymakers across party lines have constructively engaged in this process. We have organized and assembled inputs from jan sunwais (public hearings) and jan manchs (public platforms) that we conducted across several states, and discussed and debated these ideas with leaders of fourteen progressive political parties, in an effort to set benchmarks for a future common minimum programme. The overarching idea has been to try to breathe new life and spirit into the cold and self-serving logic of political and administrative processes, linking them to and informing them by grass-roots realities, fact-based research and social experience, and actionable social-scientific knowledge. And to do all of this with harmony and heart, with sincere emotion and national feeling.

In order to further disseminate these ideas, both to kick-start a national dialogue and to further build a consensus on them, we are bringing out this set of fourteen volumes highlighting innovative ideas that seek to deepen and further the promise of India. This is not an academic exercise; we do not merely spotlight structural problems, but also propose disruptive solutions to each of the pressing challenges that we collectively face. All the Her essays, though authored by top academics, technocrats, activists, intellectuals and so on, have been written purposively to be accessible to a general audience, whose creative imagination we aim to spark and whose critical feedback we intend to harness, leveraging it to further our common goals.

The inaugural volume has been specifically dedicated to our norms, to serve as a fresh reminder of our shared and shareable overlapping values and principles, collective heritage and resources. Titled Vision for a Nation: Paths and Perspectives, it champions a plural, inclusive, just, equitable and prosperous India, and is committed to individual dignity, which is the foundation of the unity and vibrancy of the nation.

The thirteen volumes that follow turn from the normative to the concrete. From addressing the problems faced by diverse communities—Adivasis, Dalit Bahujans, Other Backward Classes (OBCs)—as well as women and minorities, to articulating the challenges that we face with respect to jobs and unemployment, urbanization, healthcare and a rigged economy, to scrutinizing our higher education system or institutions more broadly, each volume details some ten specific policy solutions promising to systemically treat the issue(s), transforming the problem at a lasting structural level, not just a superficial one. These innovative and disruptive policy solutions flow from the authors' research, knowledge and experience, but they are especially characterized by their unflinching commitment to our collective normative understanding of who we can and ought to be.

The volumes that look at the concerns, needs and aspirations of Shudras, Dalits, Adivasis and women particularly look at how casteism has played havoc with India's development and stalled the possibility of the progressive transformation of Indian society. They first analyse how these sections of society have faced historical and structural discrimination against full participation in Indian spiritual, educational, social and political institutions for centuries. They also explore how the reforms that some of our epoch-making sociopolitical thinkers like Gautama Buddha, M.K. Gandhi, Jawaharlal Nehru and B.R. Ambedkar foregrounded are being systematically reversed by regressive forces and the ruling elite because of their ideological proclivities. These volumes therefore strive to address some of the most glaring social questions that India faces from a modernist perspective and propose a progressive blueprint that will secure spiritual, civil and political liberties for one and all.

What the individual volumes aim to offer, then, are navigable road maps for how we may begin to overcome the many specific challenges that we face, guiding us towards new ways of working cooperatively to rise above our differences, heal the wounds in our communities, recalibrate our modes of governance, and revitalize our institutions. Cumulatively, however, they achieve something of even greater synergy, greater import: they reconstruct that India of our imagination, of our aspirations, the India reflected in the constitutional preamble that we all surely want to be a part of.

Let us put aside that depiction of a mirror with an enemy staring back at us. Instead, together, we help to construct a whole new set of images. One where you may look at your nation and see your individual identity and dignity reflected in it, and when you look within your individual self, you may find the pride of your nation residing there.

Aakash Singh Rathore, Mridula Mukherjee, Pushparaj Deshpande
and *Syeda Hameed*

Introduction

G.N. Devy

The debate on the genesis of the social category called Adivasi
in India is not yet a settled one. Different views exist on
this question. One strong contender is that colonial rule in India
resulted in the designation of Adivasis as a distinct ethnic and social
group. It is true that European colonialism applied 'indigenous' as
an anthropological tag to numerous local communities in North
and South America, Australia and the Pacific, Africa and Asia.
However, while the idea could be applied with a much greater use
in North America and Australia, in South America, Africa and Asia,
the communities encountered by the colonial powers were far too
complex to be covered under the simple 'indigenous' tag. The rise
of terms such as 'aboriginal', 'Indians', 'indigenous' and 'tribes' in
different continents too indicates that the process of imagining 'the
other' during the extended history of colonialism was not without
complexities and grey areas. It cannot, however, be denied that the
current discourse related to the Adivasis in India owes a great deal
to its colonial history.

There is another theory on this question which likes to view
Adivasis as a social legacy inherited by us from pre-colonial times.
There are ample descriptions of forest dwellers in epics, plays,

myths and folktales, giving evidence of communities distinct from the urban and rural Indian society in existence since pre-historic times. These forest people appear in those narratives and descriptions as being outside the pale of the law, social customs, traditions and belief systems prevailing in different historical epochs in India's history. The question of whether these forest-dwelling communities emerged during the colonial times as 'tribals' too is difficult to answer in a simple affirmation or negation. The situation is quite varied. For instance, the people of Manipur and Tripura appear in the epics as the 'main people'. But during colonial times, many of them are found to be relegated to the term 'tribe'. On the other hand, many subsets of the population in Rajasthan would be placed in the category of 'out of the pale' in pre-colonial India; but they find place in non-tribal, caste-bound Indian society from the fifteenth century onwards. Given this, who exactly is 'tribal', 'Adivasi' or 'jan-jati', as a post-Independence bureaucrat may describe them, is a question quite difficult to answer.

Ever since the Schedule of Tribes was conceptualized after Independence, the question has become even more difficult. Over the last seven decades, the demand for a given community's inclusion in the Schedule has come up far too frequently and such inclusions have been made not too infrequently. Given this uncertainty related to the exact genesis of Adivasis, their ethnic characteristics and their social standing, the use of terms such as 'Adivasis' or 'Tribes' has to be understood entirely with reference to the context in which these terms get used. In the context of this book, the contributors have used the terms as indicative of the concept rather than indicative of the exact official status of communities implied in their arguments. The discussion in the essays covers a wide range of such communities, such as the ones in the North-eastern states, which are fairly distinct in many ways from the communities in the central belt of India. It includes communities from the central belt such as the Mundas, Bhils, Gonds and Santhals. It also includes the communities brought under a draconian law—the Criminal Tribes Act—in 1871 and its subsequent revisions during the colonial rule. In other words, the aim of this book is not to discuss just the officially declared jan-jatis, though they too are Adivasi almost entirely. The aim of the book is to present a perspective on the *people who are* Adivasi or tribe-like pastoralists and nomads.

It would, no doubt, be a gross oversimplification to maintain that all of the communities brought into discussion in this volume have identical issues and concerns at the centre of their hugely divergent worldviews and cultural or political discourses. Yet, making allowance for differences, it would not be far off the mark to say that their endangered identity, environment, language, gender sensitivity, belief systems, performance traditions and human rights are some of the more central issues relating to the struggles and the survival of the indigenous all over the country. The local features of these struggles vary from community to community and from state to state. However, the general narrative is fairly common. Quintessentially, this narrative refers to a colonial experience that hammered a break in the long-standing traditions of the indigenous; yet they kept close to their traditions and close also to nature, losing in the process their control over natural resources, land, rivers and forests, and continued to clash with a radically different framework of justice, ethics and spirituality. For the indigenous, invariably, there are two points in time marking their emergence: one that is traced back to a mythological time enshrined in their collective memory and expressed in their community's 'story of origin', the other that is synchronous with a colonial forest officer or beat guard setting foot on the land that was once their dominion. It is true that no established research or theory in archaeology, anthropology, genetics, cultural geography, historical linguistics, agriculture and forestry goes to show that all or any of the indigenous people have been inhabitants of the very same land where they were when colonialism made its presence felt. Probably, a very small portion of them have been associated with their present habitat since the time homo sapiens inhabited the subcontinent. There have been migrations from place to place and from one part of the continent to the other during prehistoric times. Yet, despite the prehistoric migrations, it is true that indigenous communities have been associated with their habitats for a considerably long time. The European colonial quest, the territorial and cultural invasion associated with it and the interference of alien political, ecological and belief-system-related paradigms brought a threat to the traditions that the indigenous had developed. The absence of desire on their part to accept the new paradigms and to internalize them made them stand out, be marked as 'others' not just for the colonial rulers but also for other sections of Indian society, be interpreted as 'primitive' and represented as 'indigenous'. It is common sense that the term 'indigenous', as a part of a binary, can have meaning only when there are other terms such as 'alien', 'outsiders', 'non-native' and 'colonialists'. One without the other would cease to have the meaning that it now has.

Though census exercises in different countries do not use a uniform framework, methodology and orientation, data available through the censuses carried out by various nations shows that approximately 370 million of the world's population is indigenous. The communities identified as indigenous on the basis of their location, uniqueness of tradition, social structures and community law number close to 5000 and are spread over ninety countries. Despite inadequacy in the world's knowledge about the indigenous, it is clear that their existence, environment, cultural ethos, lifestyles and values have been under relentless assault by the practices, culture and value of the rest of the world. In recognition of the threat to indigenous cultures and knowledge systems, to their land and environment, languages, livelihood and law, the United Nations came out with a Declaration on the Rights of Indigenous People, accepted by the United Nations (UN) General Assembly in September 2007. However, the UN framework has been only a normative framework and produced little impact on the situation of the indigenous. The main reason for the UN apparatus is that the indigenous are normally a small minority in any country where they exist. In the case of Adivasis in India, the situation is no different. Census data over several decades shows that their population normally amounts to 8 or 9 per cent of India's overall population. One does not have to go any further to identify the main reason for the political ineffectiveness of Adivasis in India. To be indigenous is, in our time, to be severely marginalized in economy, politics, institutionalized knowledge and institutionalized religion. The space for the indigenous is rapidly shrinking. One can illustrate this: The semi-official definition of 'Adivasi' in India is that they are 'shy'. They live in remote areas. They have their belief systems and their own languages. The year 2019 was declared by the United Nations Educational, Scientific and Cultural Organization (UNESCO) as the Year of the Indigenous Languages. There were official celebrations and academic conferences to 'celebrate' the year. However, it is a fact that several hundreds of the languages of Adivasis still kept alive by the communities are close to extinction. A comprehensive survey of languages that I had conducted of the 780 living languages in India in 2010 showed that nearly 300 languages, mainly spoken by the indigenous peoples, may disappear in the next few decades. In India, the Central government passed a law in 2008 requiring that land ownership of the tribal communities be returned to them. However, nearly half of the claims have yet to be settled and the Supreme Court of India has already asked that the families—whose land title claims have not been accepted— be evacuated. Despite legal provisions aimed at safeguarding communities and their cultures, they are diminishing and suffering an undeserving obsolescence in a world that has been vandalizing the natural resources of the earth as never before. Several decades ago, I started working with the Adivasis in Gujarat. Soon, I noticed how the rapid depletion of their forest resources had become a major cause of their pauperization. It is not as if there were not enough laws to protect their interests; but all the laws came to them as an alien system of thought and practice. The struggle to understand this alien sense of justice has taken the Adivasis such a long time that by now they are almost at the fag end of their losing battle and left with a few broken English words as their only consolation. In that sense, the forest they lost now speaks English! The perspectives brought together in this volume by persons from Adivasi communities or the ones actively engaged in the situation of Adivasis make it sufficiently useful in gaining a more than anthropological understanding of the situation of the indigenous.

If the awareness of Adivasis and their concerns is scant among the non-Adivasi population of India, knowledge about communities described as 'Denotified Tribes' is almost absent. Lest the term be misunderstood as 'some kind of Adivasis' or 'officially non-recognized Adivasis'—which is not unusual among even those who know something about Adivasis—I would like to offer the following brief description of the Denotified Tribes. During the nineteenth century, after the British had more or less secured authority over all princely states in India, they found it necessary to disarm the disbanded soldiers of the vanquished armies of Indian princes. The British also wanted to ensure safe travels in Indian states for commercial purposes. In order to accomplish the two objectives, they appointed William Henry Sleeman to detect the use of arms by unauthorized individuals. Sleeman made copious notes and listed instances of armed clashes on highways in central India. In the process, he gave rise to the idea of 'thuggee'. The idea attracted readers of his books back in England. The list of persons and their communities came to be associated with the idea of thuggee or communities that make looting and crime their profession. The 1871 Criminal Tribes Act (CTA) was based on this notion. It listed communities as 'criminal communities', implying that being born in any of those communities made one automatically criminal in tendency. The CTA provided for 'reformatory settlement', which were soft prisons. The listed communities were interned in these settlements, with severe restrictions placed on their free movement.

Sleeman's list had many flaws in it. Most of the communities had been traditionally nomadic in habit, an age-old social phenomenon in India. Members of the interned communities were put to hard labour, in most instances unpaid labour.

It is difficult to estimate as to how many perished due to the stress of labour. The members of these communities continued to live in the settlements for several generations spread over eight decades. In 1952, two years after India adopted the Constitution, the 'notified' communities were 'denotified'. They continued to be described as Denotified and Nomadic Tribes (DNT), while very few of them found a place in the official lists of jan-jatis, the 'indigenous peoples' or Adivasis. The stigma of criminality continued to stick to them despite the slight change in the label. Not being included in the lists of STs and SCs, with a few exceptions, they continued to languish without land, livelihood or access to schools and healthcare. Not having fixed addresses, their minimum rights as citizens too were not safeguarded. The stigma around their name often causes harassment from villagers and the urban population even to this day. There have been widespread incidences of mob lynching of members of the DNT communities. Governments have been generally indifferent to the plight of the DNTs as they do not form even a substantial minority, though their total population in the country is by no means insignificant. When Dr Manmohan Singh's United Progressive Alliance (UPA) government appointed me as chairman of the Technical Advisory Group for the Denotified, Nomadic and Semi-nomadic Communities, I found that the population of the DNTs could be close to seven–eight crore. That was in 2008. At present, the number may have gone up and may be close to ten crore. The Census of India has never carried out any clear counting of the DNTs. And since the numbers are not officially ascertained, the locations of these communities are not properly documented and no systematic thought has been given to their livelihood requirements and their human rights; they continue to remain in India's imagination as the invisible

nowhere people. The present volume includes an introductory
essay on the DNTs. For several decades following Independence,
'Adivasi' was an anthropomorphic 'type' cast in sentiment and piety,
or else dismissed as historical baggage worth leaving behind in India's
march to modernity and nationhood. Though the complexities
of Adivasi society received attention in scholarships related to the
theme, the popular attitude to Adivasis was severely restricted by
the acronym 'ST'. Excessive pity and excessive contempt are both
equally potent instruments of 'othering' people. It is therefore
that Archana Prasad's analysis of the class–currents within Adivasi
communities becomes important as an antidote to the 'othering'
processes. She concludes, after presenting a nuanced analysis of the
tensions and textures in Adivasi contemporary identity discourse:

> . . . the multifarious manifestations of neoliberal policies have
> also created diverse forms of Adivasi politics with different social
> basis. It is therefore important to distinguish between identity-
> based struggles which have been led by those who are situated
> within the working class and those whose motive has been to
> get incorporated within the current power structure. Further,
> the culturally exclusive character of Adivasi politics is also
> hegemonic and camouflages the inequalities within the Adivasi
> society. On the other hand, non-culturally exclusive class politics
> has had to come to terms with the persistence of identity-based
> politics by adopting a more nuanced approach towards it. This
> collaboration has been facilitated by the intensifying communal
> polarisation and economic crisis, leading to the transformation
> of Adivasi politics, both class and identity based. Such a
> development is not only positive, but also essential to take on
> an authoritarian and neoliberal government and the challenges
> that it poses to all progressive forces within the country.

It needs to be mentioned that the facts of Adivasi political expression,
cultural production and major social struggles over the last half

century, all go to show that the general perception of Adivasis and their participation in modern India's process of becoming falls woefully short of reality. The new-generation Adivasis are keen to create a more realistic view, one that is from the perspective of Adivasis. Abhay Xaxa states in clear words:

> Apart from development issues, there was also a demand for a stringent anti-conversion law which has been used as a tool to divide the Adivasi communities on the lines of religion. The communal agenda of these organisations has gradually created a fear among people who don't subscribe to the dominant discourse of assimilating the Adivasis in the Hindu fold. As a result, the harmonious relationship between various Adivasi and forest dependent communities have been broken and communal violence is also increasingly experienced in Adivasi areas.

In order to obtain this view, the UPA–II government appointed the Committee headed by Virginius Xaxa. Abhay Xaxa refers to the Xaxa Committee report and points out that:

> The panel recommended radical changes to the laws, regulations and rules to protect Adivasi communities from land alienation and to ensure their rights over resources are handed back and protected. The report also laid out an overhauled, expansive and detailed framework for providing better education, health and opportunities to tribal communities across the country. If the recommendations of the Xaxa committee are implemented, it will surely have an empowering effect on Adivasi communities.

On the other hand, N.C. Saxena's essay presents a deeply sympathetic but somewhat predictably simplified view. Dr Saxena's historically important contribution to Adivasi development and the role he played inside government bureaucracy in favour of Adivasis are of a legendary proportion. Yet, seen from an Adivasi perspective, his overview is likely to be read as slightly less than a full view of what is happening today inside the minds of Adivasi communities in India. Saxena states:

> The oppressed tribals, unlike other disadvantaged groups, generally suffer and endure their exploitation silently. In some areas, however, they have taken to armed insurgency. The middle path of agitational politics by organising bundhs, taking out processions, and putting pressure on the politicians, so successfully adopted by other groups in India to articulate their grievances, is alien to the tribals and has historically been unknown to them. Civil society needs to play a big role here, and government too should not brand all tribal activists as Maoists.

These comments need to be read together with fictional works by Mahasweta Devi in order to understand that the silence of Adivasis is not the absence of voice but rather a powerful statement which we have not yet begun grasping. The 'silence' is extremely powerfully articulated by Vikrant B.:

> . . . stunted reading of social, economic and political realities created a host of mythologies and prejudices with respect to Adivasis and tribes in India. They were perceived to be isolated, self-sufficient, animist, under-developed and backward. Seemingly harmless, these mythologies have had serious policy and political implications. For example, tribes are seen as inter-linked with castes in India, by policymakers, academics, and even in popular perception. At one level, it is perhaps necessary to denote common subalternity, so as to emphasise the State's obligation to their upliftment and empowerment. However, this manufactured equivalence

glosses over the fact that while the Dalit question is relatively
centre stage in the nation's consciousness, the Adivasi question
is not.

The last clause of this paragraph sums up the purpose of this volume.
It is, in the simplest words, to present 'the Adivasi question.' It
includes the question of Adivasis in the context of modern India,
the questioning of the nation's ideas of development by Adivasis and
also the manner in which Adivasis pose their questions within the
much-misunderstood framework of their understanding of what
democracy means. Or, in other words, the Adivasi is the question
handled by this volume, the Adivasi manner of questioning too is
its concern and the questions raised by Adivasis before the Indian
nation too are its paramount concern.

Naturally, therefore, the volume is not centred on anthropology.
It is not exactly a book of political essays. It is not a book of any
cultural history trying to present the current status of Adivasis in
India. It is different in its intent and content. It is about 'the missing
dialogue between Adivasis and those who are required to think
about them'. Therefore, the essays by Shubhranshu focusing on
broadcasting Adivasi voice, Ajay Dandekar on silent voices and
distant dreams of the Denotified communities, and Ghanshyam's
depiction of what 'republic' means to Adivasis, have been brought
together as a polyphony forming this volume. Had the intention
of this volume been somewhat different, many other essays by
historians, policy makers, anthropologists, linguists and scholars
of media and culture would have become necessary. Important as
they would be in other kinds of volumes, they would probably jar
within the very specific thematic framework of this volume. I am
glad that it has only the essays it has, neither more nor less.

This volume of essays was to be edited by Abhay Xaxa, a
promising young activist-researcher. It was most unfortunate
that we should have lost him even before his genius attained full
bloom. After his sudden and sad death, the series editors asked me

if I would bring the volume to its completion. Abhay had already identified the contributors and many of their essays were already received. My task was relatively simple. It required me to give finishing touches to the collection of essays, write an introduction to the volume and pass on the manuscript to the publishers. After I had one round of reading of the essays, I thought there was need for a couple more essays. Therefore, I requested one scholar to contribute an essay. She accepted the request despite the short time I had proposed for the submission of her essay. In the past I have written books and also conceptualized and edited other books. The sense of satisfaction in completing those works and the sense I have in completing this one differs significantly. I feel happy that a work Abhay Xaxa had conceptualized—and would probably have remained unpublished due to his early death—is seeing the light of day. My little contribution to it is my humble tribute to his memory. That a man in his seventies is paying this tribute to someone whose life was cut short while he was still in his thirties is a cruel irony of fate. I am glad that the volume is getting published. I would like to hope that it is received not just as a publication or academic exercise but as a prelude to the change that is now overdue, a change that will bring to the Denotified and Nomadic communities at least some measure of justice and human rights that they expect to get as citizens of a democratic country and to Adivasis the understanding of their distinct identity. We, the people of India, owe it to them as the indigenous people of India.

Safeguarding and Deepening the Promise of India for Adivasis

Naresh Chandra Saxena

The central region of India, despite being resource rich in terms of minerals and forests, is inhabited by the poorest people who have not benefited from social and economic development to the same extent as others. Persistent problems faced by Adivasis—land alienation, indebtedness, vanishing minor forest products from government forests and displacement from their ancestral lands—are some of the causes of their impoverishment. In addition, Adivasis have suffered because of the poor quality of governance, as government servants are reluctant to work in remote tribal areas and are often absent from their official duties. Poor implementation of existing schemes in tribal regions has meant that not only does poverty continue at an exceptionally high level for Adivasis, but the decline in poverty has been much slower for them than for other social groups, as shown in Table 1.

Table 1: Percentage of People below Poverty Line and Its Rate of Decline

Category	1993–94	2011–12	Rate of Annual Decline
Scheduled Tribe (ST)	62.6	43	1.7
Scheduled Caste (SC)	60.1	29.4	2.8
Other Backward Class (OBC)	39	20.7	2.6
Others (General)	39	12.5	3
All	45.1	21.9	2.9

(Source: Press Note on Poverty Estimates, 2011–12, Planning Commission)

While the STs living in Himachal Pradesh, Mizoram, Ladakh and the southern states are not so poor, Maharashtra and Odisha exhibited rural ST poverty rates exceeding 60 per cent in 2011–12, while Chhattisgarh, Jharkhand, Madhya Pradesh and West Bengal had poverty rates for STs exceeding 50 per cent.[1] According to the 2011 census, about half of the ST households in many central Indian districts possessed neither a mobile phone, a bicycle nor a radio.[2] As per the latest Annual Health Survey, 44 per cent of women in the age group of 18 to 59 years in Koraput, a tribal district of Odisha, had body mass index below 18.5 kg/m^2 and 80 per cent of them were anemic.[3] According to the Fourth National Family Health Survey (NFHS-4) of children under five years, malnourishment in 2015-16 was highest (Table 2) among STs.

Table 2: Malnourished Children for Various Social Groups

Social Group	Stunted (In per cent)	Wasted (In per cent)	Underweight (In per cent)
ST	43.8	27.4	45.3
SC	42.8	21.2	39.3
OBC	38.7	20.5	35.5
General	31.2	19.0	28.8

(Source: NFHS-4, 2015–16)

Widespread poverty, illiteracy, absence of safe drinking water and sanitary conditions, and ineffective coverage of national health and nutritional programmes are the major contributing factors for the dismal malnutrition indicators of tribal communities.

From the viewpoint of policy, it is important to understand that tribal communities are vulnerable not only because they are poor, assetless and illiterate compared to the general population. Often their distinct vulnerability arises from their inability to negotiate and cope with the consequences of their forced integration with the mainstream economy, society, cultural and political system from which they were historically protected as a result of their relative isolation. Post-Independence, the requirements of planned development brought with them the spectre of dams, mines, industries and roads on tribal lands. With these came the concomitant processes of displacement, both literal and metaphorical. As tribal institutions and practices were forced into uneasy existence with or gave way to the market or formal state institutions (most significantly, in the legal sphere), tribal peoples found themselves at a profound disadvantage with respect to the influx of better-equipped outsiders into tribal areas. The repercussions for the already fragile socio-economic livelihood base of the tribals—ranging from the loss of livelihoods, land alienation on a vast scale and hereditary bondage—were devastating.

What has been the impact of government policies on tribal livelihoods? Where should the Central and state governments focus to improve the situation? To answer these questions, we quote in detail from a Planning Commission document:[4]

As tribal people in India perilously, sometimes hopelessly, grapple with these tragic consequences, the small clutch of bureaucratic programmes have done little to assist the precipitous pauperisation, exploitation and disintegration of tribal communities. Tribal people respond occasionally with anger and assertion, but often also in anomie and despair, because the following persistent problems have by and large remained unattended to:

- Land alienation
- Indebtedness
- Relation with forests, and government monopoly over MFPs [minor forest products], and non-implementation of the Forest Rights Act, 2006
- Ineffective implementation of Panchayats (Extension to the Scheduled Areas) Act of 1996 (PESA, 1996) for Schedule V areas
- Involuntary displacement due to development projects and lack of proper rehabilitation
- Shifting Cultivation, such as podu
- Poor utilization of government funds and
- Poor delivery of government programmes

Land Records

The official land records are in a bad shape and have often ignored tribal occupation. For instance, in Odisha, cashew plantations were raised by the Soil Conservation Department on 1,20,000 hectares of 'Government Wastelands' in Schedule V areas. In many cases such lands in the past were under cultivation by tribals, but their rights were not recorded. When settlement took place, tribals—because of their ignorance—were not in a position to get their possessions recorded, and thus the land was recorded as government land and the poor tribals were described as encroachers even on lands which were cultivated by their ancestors. These cashew plantations, raised on land that supported the livelihood needs of tribals, were handed over for management to the Odisha State Cashew Development Corporation. As the corporation could not run profitably, it started giving annual leases for harvesting of cashew crops to private parties through open auctions. This is land reform in reverse! It is ironical that these plantations—that deprived the tribals of their possession—were funded by a scheme called the 'Economic Rehabilitation of the Rural Poor'.

The Ministry of Tribal Affairs should do a quick study of the loopholes in various state laws and come up with model legislation for both: restoration of alienated lands as well as to check further transfer. Amendments in the Madhya Pradesh Land Revenue Code, 1959 through Section 170(B) of the code may serve as a good model. It instituted suo moto responsibility of the revenue court to enquire into all transactions from tribal to non-tribal, even without an application from the tribal. The burden of proof was shifted to the non-tribal to prove that fraud did not take place and the presumption of the court supported the legal rights of the original tribal landowner. The appearance of advocates without permission · has also been debarred in these proceedings. There is provision for only a single appeal to the collector. However, non-tribals have been able to delay proceedings by resorting to revisions. One must plug such loopholes too.

Section 211 of the Uttar Pradesh Zamindari Abolition and Land Reforms Act, applicable to usurpation of tribal lands by outsiders in the tarai lands (now mostly in Uttarakhand), may also serve as a model. It reads as follows:

'211. (1) Where any land held by a tenure-holder belonging to a Scheduled Tribe is in occupation of any person other than such tenure-holder, the Assistant Collector may, suo motu or on the application of such tenure-holder put him in possession of such land after evicting the occupant and may, for that purpose use or cause to be used such force as may be considered necessary, anything to the contrary contained in this Act notwithstanding.

(2) Where any person, after being evicted from any land under sub-section (1), re-occupies the land or any part thereof without any lawful authority, he shall be punishable with imprisonment for a term which may extend to three years but which shall not be less than six months and also with a fine which may extend to three thousand rupees but which shall not be less than one thousand rupees.

(3) Any court convicting a person under sub-section (2) may make an order to put the tenure-holder in possession of such land

or any part thereof and such person shall be liable to eviction without prejudice to any other action that may be taken against him under any other law for the time being in force.

(4) Every offence punishable under sub-section (2) shall be cognizable and non-bailable.'

Passing of such laws by the state governments should be accompanied by simplification of judicial procedures, constitution of special courts and sensitization of district officials. The progress of restoration of land should be carefully monitored by an assessment of total area alienated, fixation of annual targets for the states and its supervision by a high-level empowered committee chaired by the Cabinet Secretary, with at least two members in this committee from civil society with experience of working in tribal areas. Such a committee should meet at least once a quarter and its minutes should be kept on the ministry's website.

Moreover, legal aid should be provided to tribal communities so all pending land disputes are monitored and settled immediately and tribals do not face constant harassment from non-tribals or revenue and other departments. Regular updating of land records, proper and regular conduct of jamabandi and display of revenue details at the village level should also help to achieve this objective. Sample surveys should be done to assess how many tribals have legal pattas with them, and how this number has changed over the years.

Displacement

Adivasis have generally been harmed by displacement due to industrialization. Nearly 85 lakh tribals had been displaced until 1990 on account of some mega project, reservation of forests as National Parks, etc. Tribals constitute 8 per cent of the population but are 55 per cent of the total displaced people in the country.[5] Cash payment does not really compensate them for the difficulties they experience in their living style and ethos.

The Niyamgiri victory against Vedanta and Sterlite—two major corporations—was a major triumph of a people's movement that had the support of an international campaign to protect the Kondhs, classified as a particularly vulnerable tribal group (PVTG). Their community rights to the forests in and around the Niyamgiri Hills in Odisha were in jeopardy. The findings of the N.C. Saxena Committee revealed that the state government and Vedanta and its associate companies had engaged in both acts of omission and commission. The mining company had violated the Forest Conservation Act by illegally occupying twenty-six hectares of village forest land in the area. It had brazenly embarked on construction activity to expand its production capacity at its aluminum refinery complex from one to six million tonne per annum without obtaining clearance under the Environment Protection Act. The refinery was also obtaining its ore from fourteen mines, eleven of which did not have environmental clearance.[6] The Supreme Court judge noted that '. . . the de facto dependence on the Niyamgiri forests for the past several decades can be ignored by the central and state governments only at the cost of betrayal of the promise of inclusive growth and justice and dignity for all Indians'.[7] But as the *Economic and Political Weekly* points out, 'For every Niyamgiri there are hundreds of other cases where corporate interests, and the state and the central governments have colluded to trample on the lives of local people'.[8]

Today, project-affected people are no longer in a mood to suffer passively. Large-scale protests by tribals against major mining companies like Vedanta Alumina in Kalahandi and TISCO in Kalinganagar in Odisha are examples in the long history of resistance to mining. Consequently, there have been growing protests and militancy, leading to tensions, conflict and violence. Unsatisfactory arrangements for tribal rehabilitation and resettlement create opposition to acquisition of land and ultimately the costs involved in delayed acquisition of land are much more than costs incurred in case of satisfactory compensation and rehabilitation. A well-intended, liberal and comprehensive resettlement and rehabilitation policy is therefore required not only to protect the interests of the displaced or adversely affected people, but also in public interest to ensure quick acquisition and faster access to such land.

The clause in the new 2013 law (Right to Fair Compensation and Transparency in Land Acquisition, Rehabilitation and Resettlement Act)—requiring consent of at least 70 per cent of project-affected people—is highly welcome. It is unfortunate that Gujarat in 2016 diluted the Land Acquisition Act and did away with social impact assessment and consent clauses for acquisition of land for public purposes, industrial corridors and public–private partnership projects.

Often, land values go up after acquisition and the original owners feel cheated when they find that their land after a few years is being sold for ten times the price that was paid to them. Therefore, whenever land acquired by government is transferred to an individual or a company for a consideration, 20 per cent of the appreciated value should be given to the original landowner. In addition, the government must ensure that displaced tribal families have a standard of living superior to the one before their displacement and have a sustainable income above the poverty line. Gains to the displaced should be of the same scale as the project beneficiaries.

Even under the 2013 law, affected households are not compensated when forest or common lands and water bodies are resumed by government and passed on to private bodies, on the plea that these are government lands and require no acquisition. In the absence of any protection, the poorest people as users of common lands and forests and slum dwellers are thus deprived of their livelihoods without any rehabilitation benefits. This is particularly relevant in view of the state governments' reluctance to implement the community clauses of the Forest Rights Act.

Forest Policy

There is much evidence to show that the tribals' access to forests for meeting their basic subsistence needs has deteriorated in the last seventy years and that this is fairly widespread. Some of the processes which have caused this are anti-tribal policies such as the forest policy of 1952, preference for man-made plantations in place of mixed forests, diversion of non-timber forest products (NTFPs) and forests to industries, nationalization of NTFPs and exploitation by government agencies and contractors in the marketing of NTFPs. Tribal women in Rayagada in Odisha were once arrested in 1995 and jailed for keeping brooms in their homes!

Policies related to MFPs in the states are often dictated by the desire to maximize state revenues and not the welfare of gatherers, who are often tribal women. The revenue interest of Odisha can be judged by the fact that during the period 1989–2001, the state government earned revenues of Rs 7.52 billion from kendu leaves (KL). The total wages earned by KL pickers during the same period was only Rs 3.87 billion.[9] The high incidence of royalties on KL needs to be contrasted with the royalties collected on a major mineral, where labour is organized, e.g., royalties are Rs 30 per tonne on bauxite, but a whopping Rs 12,000 per tonne on KL![10]

Forests Rights Act (FRA) was a landmark legislation enacted in 2006 to correct the 'historic injustice done to forest-dwelling communities', mostly tribals, who were cultivating/occupying forest land and using forest produce for ages but had no tenurial security, as their rights of occupation and usage were not recorded during the settlement process. Although counting both individual and community rights, more than 1.8 million titles have been issued covering 5.5 million hectares,[11] in many places the area settled with the forest dwellers is much less than their occupation; boundaries of the settled area are not demarcated and rejections are being done without assigning reasons. The picture is also dismal when it comes to recognizing community forest rights (CFR). Granting of titles cannot be considered the end of the story. If the objective is to strengthen the livelihoods of forest dwellers, state governments need to improve productivity of assigned land by linking it with soil conservation works and the Mahatma Gandhi National Rural

Employment Guarantee Act (MGNREGA) funds and assist in marketing of harvested products.

About 23 lakh applications have been rejected.[12] It is likely that many such cases were genuine but got rejected on flimsy grounds, such as caste certificate not included or proof of seventy-five years of residence needed by non-tribal forest dwellers not attached, etc. The Supreme Court had in February 2019 directed all states to re-examine such cases and inform the court.

Similarly, in addition to recognizing community rights, the government should actively improve the livelihoods of forest dwellers through higher production of gatherable biomass and better opportunities for its collection and marketing. MFPs play an important role in the economic well-being of the forest-dwelling communities. Unfortunately, overall production of MFPs (except tendu leaves) has fallen rapidly due to the Forest Department's preference for planting species such as teak (in place of sal), which yield no recurrent products for gathering. Therefore, silvicultural practices should be radically changed to boost the production of gatherable biomass and not merely timber. We need crown-based forestry, not trunk-based forestry that mostly benefits contractors.

Moreover, important MFPs continue to be 'nationalized', that is, these can be sold only to government agencies. Then, many state governments have created new rights of industrialists through long-term agreements to supply forest products at a low price, bypassing local peoples' rights and privileges. Sale of MFPs is usually governed by a complex set of rules and regulations. A limited number of buyers thus operate under monopolistic conditions. For instance, in Tamil Nadu, an area with an abundance of *Prosopis juliflora* (an excellent coppicing shrub with high calorific value), charcoal producers have to obtain a certificate of origin from Forest Officers. This results in constant harassment. Over-regulation and complex procedures hurt value addition. Licences have been done away with for large industries in India, but not for tiny and cottage industries based on forest raw material.

If farmers are free to sell their wheat and paddy in the open market, why restrict tribals from doing so for MFPs? States should attract tribals by paying them remunerative price support rather than coerce them to sell to government agencies.

Therefore, in addition to guaranteeing that FRA is implemented in letter and spirit, one would have to address three interrelated issues for ensuring that tribal livelihoods are supported and enriched by MFPs (Saxena, 2018):

1. How to increase MFP production, while sustaining the resource
2. How to improve access of the poor to MFPs
3. How to maximize their incomes through marketing

Rather than be a monopoly buyer of NTFPs, the government should adopt market-friendly policies, facilitate private trade and act as a watchdog rather than eliminate the trade. It should encourage local bulking, storage and processing and bring large buyers in touch with gatherers to reduce the number of layers of intermediaries. Lastly, it should provide minimum support price, as is done for wheat and paddy farmers.

Education

An important difference between SCs and STs is language. While SCs speak the same language as the dominant group, STs often speak a different dialect or even language, with their children having the handicap of being taught at schools in a language they do not understand, resulting in higher dropout rates. This is one of the most serious handicaps facing the tribes.

Most teachers teaching in Adivasi schools are non-Adivasis who tend to view Adivasi language, culture and social practices as being inferior to theirs. Psychologically, this has a strong negative impact on children, which again contributes to their dropping out of school. One way of tackling this problem would be to change the way Adivasi communities are being educated. For instance, if textbooks were to be prepared in the language of the Adivasis to express their culture, worldview and concepts, it would make it easier for Adivasi children to begin learning, since they would be already familiar with the language and content of the textbooks. It would also mean that they would have to learn only two skills, reading and writing. In time, they could gradually begin to learn the language of the state, which would put them on a par with non-Adivasi students.

Governance

It is unfortunate that the Ministry of Tribal Affairs (MoTA) does not give sufficient attention to the important problems of the tribals on the plea that many of these, such as land alienation, displacement, forest policy, and the Panchayats (Extension to the Scheduled Areas) Act or PESA have not been allotted to it. Even then, the ministry should play a more active role in addressing these issues by pursuing them with the ministries concerned, where tribal concerns are often neglected. An effective monitoring mechanism should be set up to bring out the dismal picture of tribal areas that would put pressure on sectoral ministries and states to improve their programmes and implementation.

When MoTA was set up in 2001, it was expected that it would take a holistic view of tribal problems and coordinate the activities of all other ministries that deal with the subjects impinging on tribal livelihoods. The new ministry, however, took a minimalist view of its responsibility and reduced itself to dealing with only such schemes (such as distribution of scholarships and grants to NGOs) for which budgets are provided. Such an ostrich-like attitude defeats the purpose for which the ministry was created.

MoTA does not even monitor whether basic services in education, health or nutrition are reaching tribal hamlets. The ministry should develop meaningful partnerships with advocacy organizations that could produce credible and evidence-based reports with a view to engage with other ministries that oversee various programmes such as the Integrated Child Development Services, National Health Mission, Public Distribution System (PDS), etc., in a way that such programmes reach the Adivasis. Even in areas where there is Naxalite presence or in very remote and apparently inaccessible areas, civil society organizations can be funded to run mobile clinics and feeding centres. Clearly, it is a lack of will on the part of the administration that needs to be set right first.

Tribal Leadership

One of the main factors behind the success of Dalits in India has been excellent leadership provided by the SC community, which has unfortunately not been the case for the Scheduled Tribes. Whereas the Scheduled Castes can boast of having produced leaders and administrators such as B.R. Ambedkar and Jagjivan Ram in the past and K.R. Narayanan, Buta Singh, Ram Vilas Paswan, Kanshi Ram and Mayawati in more recent times, it is hard to find any of national stature from the Scheduled Tribe category. A few civil servants, such as B.D. Sharma and S.R. Sankaran, tried to alleviate their conditions, but such efforts could not be sustained for lack of institutional support.

The oppressed tribals, unlike other disadvantaged groups, generally suffer and endure their exploitation silently. In some areas, however, they have taken to armed insurgency. The middle path of agitational politics by organizing bundhs, taking out processions and putting pressure on politicians, so successfully adopted by other groups in India to articulate their grievances, is alien to the tribals and has historically been unknown to them. Civil society needs to play a big role here and the government too should not brand all tribal activists as Maoists.

Adivasis are unable to put democratic pressure on the bureaucratic and political system from which they were historically protected as a result of their relative isolation. A few respond occasionally with anger and assertion, go underground and get attracted to Naxals. Unfortunately for them, Indian history in the last 150 years shows that terrorism and violent insurgency have never succeeded in achieving their aims (the creation of Mizoram may be the only exception). On the contrary, overground agitational strategies have been the most successful, leading to the creation of new states and changes in government policy (such as the declaration of the Emergency in 1975 due to the Jayaprakash Narayan movement). Arvind Kejriwal is the latest example of success in agitational politics.

What about Naxals? Though in a few exceptional cases Naxals have been able to improve tribal livelihoods, such as getting minimum wages for the *tendu* leaf gatherers in Andhra Pradesh, they have mostly degenerated into a terrorist outfit with little impact on the day-to-day agony of the local population. In the 1970s and early 1980s, the Naxalite movement may have had ideological base, today they are just brigands. The poor tribals are often subjected to physical violence by both Maoists and state forces; they even get deprived of educational and health facilities or access to PDS on the ground that the area has become unapproachable for normal 'development' efforts of the administration.

Although there are some activist organizations who speak for the tribals openly through social media and do advocacy to stop their exploitation, their number and effectiveness is limited. They have neither been able to reduce the lack of trust between the people and the State, nor improve governance in the tribal belts. We need more democratic, well informed and overground grassroots organizations for effective advocacy both in policy and implementation. The poor Adivasis are today trapped between Maoists on the one hand and armed forces on the other. Mere sympathy for the Naxals is self-defeating as the path of underground violence is not the answer for tribal problems and will not end tribal oppression.

Genuine grassroots organizations and the tribals themselves must learn—from the Shiv Sena and Kejriwal—the strategy of agitational politics.

Tribal Development in Fifth Schedule Areas: Affirmative Action or Unequal Exchange?

Virginius Xaxa

Introduction

It was during the British rule that tribes were brought under the same legal and administrative structure that existed for the larger Indian society. Undeniably, the structure introduced by the British was alien to non-tribals as well, but not to the extent that it was for tribes. Non-tribals were consistently part of the state structure and hence familiar with its rules and operations. They were also part of the administration that ran the state. Tribes, on the other hand, neither had experience with administration, nor of alien power and authority. In a way, they were lords and masters of the territory they held or occupied. They lost this under the British when they came under laws, rules and regulations relating to land, forest, crimes and punishment that were alien to them. In some parts of tribal India, the British imposed upon the tribes the notion of private property and landlordism in place of lineage or community-based ownership of land. Revenue collectors and administrative officials were converted into owners and landlords. This led to large-scale eviction of tribes from their land and installation of non-tribes in their place, as the latter were considered to be better agriculturists and hence could pay higher rent. In places where tribes still had control over land, massive transfers to non-tribes took place through measures such as fraud, deceit, mortgage, etc. Since tribes had no practice of record keeping as they did not read or write, non-tribes took advantage of them by forging evidence and documents in their favour. The local administration, which was manned by the non-tribes, worked hand in glove with their ethnic kind to ensure a smooth transfer of land. Meanwhile, the colonial state took upon itself rights over the forest, thereby denying tribes the right to collect fuel and other daily necessities for which they were heavily dependent on the forest.[1] These processes caused havoc in tribal societies. They lost autonomy and control over land and forest. This, in turn, drastically affected their access to livelihood.

Their response to this loss of access to livelihood and autonomy invariably took the form of armed struggle. In fact, all through the late eighteenth and nineteenth centuries, the early encounter of the British with these groups or communities, which later came to be described as tribes, was characterized by a series of revolts and rebellions. Prominent among them at this early phase were the revolts of the Pahariya Sirdars (1778), the Tamar Revolt (1789, 1794–95), tribal revolt (1807–08) and agrarian tribal revolts (1811, 1817, 1820). However, it was the revolts that took place after the Great Kol Insurrection of 1831–32 that received wide attention. Prominent among these revolts are the Bhumij Revolt (1832–33), the Santhal Rebellion (1855–57), the Kherwar/Sardari Movement (1858–95) and the Birsa Munda Movement (1895–1990).[2] All these revolts occurred in what was then referred to as the Santhal Pargana and Chotanagpur regions of British India.

Birth of Scheduled Areas

In response to these resistance movements, the British administration toyed with the idea of a suitable administrative set-up for the agitated tribes. After much experimenting, it came up with 'arrangements' different from those in the non-tribal areas. This was reflected in Regulation X of 1822 which introduced the concept of a non-regulated system for the administration of 'difficult areas'. This meant that the difficult areas would not be governed by regulations as was the practice in other areas under the British. Rather, the executive would administer the region as per the discretion authority of the governor-general in council. The genealogy of the fifth and the sixth can be traced to this system in force in different parts of British India.[3] What is now known as the tribal population inhabited most of these difficult and inaccessible areas.

The Government of India Act, 1870 allowed the governor-general to legislate separately for the difficult areas, which later came to be described as backward areas. The distinct legislative and executive measures were aimed primarily at safeguarding the interests of the tribes. From 1874, backward/tribal areas came to be governed by the Scheduled District Act. As per this Act, the government was required to notify which laws were to be enforced in the Scheduled areas/districts. Such provisions continued under the Government of India Act, 1919, which gave power to Indians with regard to 'self-governance' on certain issues. It may be noted that enactments made by legislatures were not directly applicable in tribal areas, unless so desired by the executive authority. Even under the Government of India Act 1935, the tribal areas declared as 'excluded' and 'partially excluded' were not brought under the purview of the federal or provincial legislatures. As to whether laws were to be extended in full or in part or with modification was left to the judgement of the executive authority. In the exercise of this authority, maintaining peace was the most important consideration.

The British initiative towards a system of administration for the tribes that was somewhat distinct from that of the larger Indian population did provide the former some space; they were allowed to be governed by their own traditions and customary practices. Such legal and administrative arrangements, however, did not

restrict the movement of population from outside the tribal areas
into tribal areas, except in the frontiers of the North-eastern region
where the inner line permit system was introduced. Rather, there
was now a greater movement of people from outside into tribal
areas. This was because tribal areas saw further expansion of roads,
railways and colonial administration, leading to greater penetration
of the market. The credit, land and labour market came to play
a dominant role in tribal areas, with far reaching implications on
their society. Hence, in tribal regions other than the frontiers of
the North-east, population movement as well as the alienation of
land from tribes to non-tribes continued through fraud, deceit and,
more importantly, through debt.

Despite this, unlike the early phase of contact which was
marked by revolt and rebellion, there were fewer such struggles
towards the latter half of British rule. This may be mainly to do
with the consolidation of the non-tribal population in tribal areas
and the upsurge of the freedom movement that brought diverse
groups and communities under one umbrella. The widespread
struggle against the British, in which tribes also participated, seems
to have diverted the inner contradiction and conflict between
tribes and non-tribes. The tribal population by now had not only
reconciled to the presence of outsiders but had also begun to see
them as superiors and begun to emulate them and their lifestyles.
This was evident in the process of Hinduization and Sanskritization
that set in from the beginning of the twentieth century. This is not
to say there was no discontent. Rather, with the momentum of the
freedom movement, agrarian and forest issues came to the forefront
among the tribes but with a difference. This time, the movements
were part of the larger mobilization process of civil disobedience
or non-cooperation movements launched by the Congress or other
nationalist leaderships. The agrarian movement not only took the
form of non-cooperation and civil disobedience against the colonial
state, but also of struggle and resistance against exploitation and
oppression of the landlords. The latter were mobilized primarily

by left-wing political parties both in the colonial and post-colonial periods. Such struggles were aimed broadly at the security of tenure, reduction of rent, increased share of produce, etc. In these, tribals aligned with other exploited classes of the agrarian society.

Alongside this movement, discontent began to take another form towards this phase, which was modern and forward-looking. It was the beginning of a movement for separate states/homelands for tribes. Such stirrings were taking roots among the Bhils, Gonds, Mundas, Santhals, Oraons and other tribal groups of peninsular India. In North-east India too, such demands had begun to be articulated.

Tribes in Post-Independence India

The British rule thus brought tribes and non-tribes under one political and administrative authority. With some exceptions, they were subjected to the same laws, rules, regulations and administration. The same was the case in the economic sphere. Through land, labour, credit and commodity markets, they were all brought under a single economic order. Tribes thus came to be part of the same political and economic system that the larger Indian society was a part of. However, the position tribes came to occupy in the new politico-administrative system was one characterized by the steady erosion of their control and access to land, forest and other resources. Both the colonial administration and non-tribal population, especially traders, merchants and moneylenders, were responsible for this. Tribes had thus to go through the process of twin colonialism, one of the British rule and administration and the other of the non-tribal population. Tribes who previously had control over land, forest and other resources and enjoyed the autonomy of governance, got pushed to the margin of the new political and economic system. There was thus the process of integration/inclusion of tribes into the larger system under colonial rule, but this came to be intertwined with the process of exclusion in the form of loss of access and control over livelihood (economic rights) and in the determination of their own lives.

Many provisions were made in the Indian Constitution to draw tribals from their existing isolation and social backwardness and integrate them into the larger Indian society. In order to ensure their integration and build up an inclusive society, tribals were, to begin with, given the same citizenship rights and status as those accorded to members of the larger Indian society. Citizenship entitles an individual full membership of a community, at least in principle. Citizenship rights, in the words of T.H. Marshall[4], comprised three components: civil, political and social. Civil rights are composed of rights necessary for individual freedom. They entail the right to liberty of the person and the right to freedom of speech, thought and faith. The right to own property and the right to justice are other important components. Right to justice means the right to be treated in terms of equality with others in regard to defence and assertion of one's own rights. Political rights mean the right to participate in the exercise of political power as a member of a body vested with political authority, such as Parliament or its counterparts at the regional and local levels. It also means the right to participate in the process whereby members exercising political authority are elected. Social rights mean the right to a modicum of economic welfare and security and the right to social heritage, which means the right to live the life of a civilized being according to standards prevailing in society.[5]

Affirmative Action Programme: What the State Has Given

In addition to the above, tribals along with Dalits were given special rights that other citizens were not entitled to. The special rights granted to them were meant to compensate for the disability they suffered for centuries either due to systemic discrimination (in the case of the Dalits) or historical isolation (in the case of tribes) and thereby ensure their effective enjoyment of citizenship rights enshrined in the Constitution. The special rights come closer to what may be termed as social rights. Special rights meant for tribals have been of various kinds. There have been rights aimed at safeguarding and protecting the interests of the tribal people. There are rights aimed at ensuring participation in state institutions. Towards fulfillment of these rights, a certain percentage of seats were reserved for them in state institutions such as Parliament and state legislatures, governments and institutions of higher learning. The rights so provided in the Constitution are more popularly known as the reservation facilities. Finally, there are provisions in the Constitution that aim to uplift the tribal people from their social backwardness and underdevelopment. The special treatment given to a certain category of people for their welfare, to protect their interests and promote their development may be broadly termed as the affirmative action programme in India.

Affirmative action programmes are interventions that aim primarily to address the issues faced by disadvantaged groups. Possible interventions, according to Myron Weiner,[6] are broadly of four types. One is a wide range of policies that aim to reverse social inequality, but which are racially/ethnically neutral. The second concerns policies directed at eliminating barriers to entry to jobs, universities, etc. The third type aims to improve the quality of the pool from which individuals are recruited. Reservation for the disadvantaged is the other possible intervention.

All of these possible interventions in different measures have been at work in the context of India. However, what has received wide attention and generated public debate is reservation. The debate on reservation has not so much been on political reservation but on reservation in government employment and admission to institutions of higher learning, especially medical and technological institutions. Reservations in employment and educational institutions have been at work for about fifty years. Tribes have no doubt taken advantage of these provisions. This is evident from the fact that they are now found at all levels of government service. It is a different story that in terms of their share or quota, the position is far from adequate, especially at the upper echelon of government service. In fact, even by 1999, the share of the tribes in classes I and II Central government services, for example, stood at a mere 3.39 per cent and 3.35 per cent respectively. Even in the case of Classes III (6.07 per cent) and IV (7 per cent) services, the percentage fell short of the stipulated 7.5 per cent.[7] What is important to note here is that the tribals are yet to approximate the quota stipulated for them. The scenario is the same in the sphere of higher educational institutions. According to the Higher Education Statistics for 2010–11, Scheduled Tribe enrolment in higher education constituted a mere 4.39 per cent of the total tribal population of 104 million as per the 2011 census in the country.[8] It is to be noted that concern and urgency to fill the stipulated quota is much stronger in Central government services than at the state level. Unfortunately, data at state levels are not easily forthcoming.

The inability of the state to fill the quota is, however, not considered a violation of the rights enshrined in the Constitution. This is because firstly, necessary measures have been taken in pursuit of the rights enshrined in the Constitution. Secondly, the extension of reservation to candidates from the category is not automatic. Rather, it is contingent upon certain conditions or prerequisites like minimum qualifications or skills, which are in general principles stipulated in the Constitution itself (Article 335). Thirdly, even though such rights have been given to the tribes, they can avail of it only as individuals. As an individual, one can secure access to it only under certain conditions. There is, hence, an inherent difficulty in challenging the negligence or indifference of the state in the court of law.

The debate in India on reservations has been so intense that attention to other forms of affirmative policies/interventions pursued by the Indian state have been completely glossed over both by critics as well as beneficiaries of reservation. Critics have argued that rather than pursuing the system of reservation, the state must focus on capability building of disadvantaged sections, such as the Scheduled Castes and Scheduled Tribes. Indeed, those opposed to the reservation policy do not altogether rule out an affirmative policy that is aimed at enabling the disadvantaged to acquire required skills and abilities. Needless to say, the filling of quotas in jobs and educational institutions is itself contingent upon acquiring certain qualifications and skills for which special programmes for the disadvantaged— scholarship, freeship, book grants, hostel facilities, remedial classes, etc.,—do exist. Yet no serious attempt has been made to understand the way these measures have worked and the impact they have had on the disadvantaged. The question is, how effective and adequate have these affirmative action programmes been?

Since the Tenth Five Fear Plan, the schemes of post-matric scholarship, book bank and upgradation of merit (remedial and special coaching) have been combined. In the Tenth Five Year Plan, fund allocation for the above-mentioned schemes stood at Rs 383.19 crore. For upgradation of merit, against the revised allocation of Rs 83 lakh, Rs 77 lakh were released to state/union territory (UT) governments. The number of students who benefited from it were a mere 512 in 2003–04. The grants in aid released under the book bank scheme were Rs 72 lakh in 2001–02, Rs 139.98 lakh in 2002-03 and Rs 63.43 lakh in 2003-04. There were 3492 beneficiaries in 2001–02, 10,177 in 2002–03 and 7426 in 2003–04, respectively.[9] As for post-matric scholarship, the grants in aid released were Rs 667.82 lakh in 2001–02, Rs 515.86 lakh in 2002-03 and Rs 657.95 lakh in 2003-04. The actual beneficiaries were 6,01,759 in 2001–02, 6,37,241 in 2002–03, and 7,35,019 in 2003–04.[10]

In addition to the above, there have been other forms of affirmative action programmes. These programmes are geared towards improving the economic and social condition of the tribal people. The assumption was that the improvement in their economic and social well-being would help them take advantage of the benefits extended for them by the state. To this end, special considerations were made for the welfare and development of the tribal people and special allocation of resources were set aside in the plan outlay. This was evident in the very first Five Year Plan, wherein it was stated that general development programmes be so designed as to adequately address the needs of the backward classes and that special provisions be used for securing their additional and more intensified development. Accordingly, the community development programme approach—the general approach to development in India—was reoriented keeping in mind the special problems of the tribal people. This approach continued till the Fourth Five Year Plan. Since it failed to serve the interests of the tribal people, a new approach in the form of a tribal sub-plan was adopted in the Fifth Five Year Plan, which continues till date.

I shall explore later if there have really been, in the true sense of the term, affirmative action programmes for tribes in India.

A number of affirmative action programmes have been taken up by the state. The effectiveness of these programmes, however, rests on the allocation of resources. Following the introduction of the reservation policy in post-Independence India, 7.5 per cent of seats were earmarked for the Scheduled Tribes in political institutions, state employment and higher education. The size of the reservation was fixed in keeping with the size of the tribal population of the time. But plan allocations for their development have invariably fallen far short of their population size, which has undergone an increase in the course of time. In fact, till the Fourth Five Year Plan, the plan allocation has been less than 1 per cent of the total plan outlay. To be more precise, the plan outlay was 1.04 per cent in the first (1951–56), 0.96 per cent in the second (1956–61), 0.75 per cent in the third (1961–66) and 0.5 per cent in the fourth plan period (1969–74).[11] As mentioned earlier, a new strategy in the form of the tribal sub-plan was adopted in the fifth plan (1974–78). That resulted in an unprecedented increase in plan allocation for tribal development. Thus, the inception of the tribal sub-plan strategy saw an increase from Rs 1157.67 crore (3 per cent) in the fifth plan (1974–78) to Rs 3640.25 crore (3.7 per cent) in the sixth plan (1980–85), and Rs 6744.85 crore (3.8 per cent) in the seventh plan (1985–1990).[12] The eighth plan (1992-97) saw a plan allocation of Rs 22,409.65 crore, which constituted 5.2 per cent of the total allocation. However, in the very next plan of 1997–2002, though there was an increase in total outlay viz. Rs 32,087.26 crore, it constituted only 3.7 of the total plan allocation.[13]

And yet the tribal sub-plan strategy has not been able to bring about any perceptible improvement of the situation in tribal areas. A number of factors seem to account for this shoddy state of affairs. Firstly, the resources earmarked for tribal development, while they have frequently increased, were far from adequate. The plan allocation has hardly ever gone beyond 3.7 per cent. The only exception was the eighth plan period when the allocation was at 5.2 per cent of the total outlay (Govt. of India 2001, Suresh 2014). Given the inadequate funds earmarked for tribal development, especially in the first four five-year plan periods, could anything tangible have been expected with respect to tribal affirmative action programmes?

Provisions under the Fifth Schedule

The affirmative action programmes were meant to be pursued alongside a distinct administration and control provided under the provision of the Fifth Schedule of the Constitution. The Fifth Schedule makes provisions for administration and control of scheduled areas and Scheduled Tribes. Under this, there is a provision for the executive power of the state to make a report to the President regarding the administration of scheduled areas and the executive power of the Union is to give directions to the state as to the administration of the said areas. The executive power of the state, viz. the governor, has the power to direct through a public notification that an Act of Parliament or state legislature shall not apply to the scheduled area or any part thereof in the state or shall apply, subject to such exceptions and modifications as may be specified in the notification. Also, any direction given may have a retrospective effect. Further, the governor is empowered to make regulations for the peace and good governance of such areas in the state, especially with respect to: (1) prohibition or restriction of transfer of land by or among members of the Scheduled Tribes, (2) regulating the allotment of land to members of the Scheduled Tribes, (3) regulating the carrying on of business by persons who lend money to the members of Scheduled Tribe in such areas. Further, in making any such regulations, the governor may repeal or amend any act of Parliament/Legislature or any existing law which is applicable in the area in reference. All of this, the governor can do only after consultation with the Tribal Advisory Council.[14]

However, these provisions of control are never complied with, both in letter and spirit. The governors of the Fifth Schedule states hardly exercised the constitutional power vested in them to examine if laws and regulations framed by the Union or the state have been in consonance with the safeguards provided in the Constitution. They are mandated, as per the Constitution, to submit an annual report to the President on the condition of the tribal population in the respective states. However, year after year, governors have hardly discharged this duty. The Tribal Advisory Council provided for in the Constitution has generally been constituted, but its presence has been notional. They have hardly played an effective role in safeguarding the interests of the tribal population. This is evident from the discussion that follows.

What the State Has Taken

- **Land Alienation and Displacement**
  There were other interventions of much greater magnitude and scale than the ones discussed above that offset all that was desired to be achieved by the affirmative action programme. These interventions were detrimental to the interest of the

tribal people and affected their access to the affirmative action programme. They are steadily losing control over access to land, forest and other resources due to state-sponsored projects of national development on the one hand and alienation of land from tribes to non-tribes on the other. Between 1951 and 1990, a little over 21 million people are estimated to have been displaced by development projects (dams, mines, industries and wildlife sanctuaries) in India. Of the total displaced population, over sixteen million have been displaced by dams and about 2.6 and 1.3 million by mines and industries respectively. A little over one million have been displaced by other projects, wildlife sanctuaries being the most important among them. Of the total displaced, as many as 8.54 million have been enumerated as tribals. They have thus come to constitute as large as 40 per cent of the displaced population, though they comprise less than 8 per cent of the total population. Their share in the displacement from projects such as mines, wildlife sanctuaries and dams has been to the tune of over 52, 75 and 38 per cent respectively. It is only with respect to industrial and other unspecified projects that the size of their share does not exceed 25 per cent. And yet, even here the proportion is much higher than the proportion of their population to the total population of the country. Of over 21 million displaced, only 5.4 million have been resettled, out of which 2.12 million are stated to be tribals. This means that only about 24.8 per cent of displaced tribals had been rehabilitated.[15] For a very large chunk of the population, rehabilitation still remains an elusive phenomenon.

Further, land alienation from tribes to non-tribes, an endemic phenomenon for centuries, continues on a wide scale even to this day. As per information available with the Union Ministry of Rural Development in January 1999, 4,65,000 cases of alienation of tribal land covering an area 917 thousand acres have been registered in the states of Andhra

Pradesh, Assam, Bihar, Jharkhand, Gujarat, Himachal Pradesh, Karnataka, Madhya Pradesh, Maharashtra, Odisha, Rajasthan and Tripura.[16] Interestingly, with three exceptions, all are Fifth Schedule states. As per cases filed under state laws for the restoration of alienated land, the annual report of 2007–08 records 5,06,307 cases of land alienation involving 9,02,417 acres of land.[17]

- **Forest**

Prior to the introduction of the colonial forest policy, tribals were virtually the lords of the forest, enjoying rights and privileges over it. The colonial forest policy was oriented more towards revenue and profit than conservation. Hence the reclamation of forest for cultivation land, expansion of roads and railways, exploitation of mineral resources and industrial growth assumed the form of a key economic activity under colonial rule. Needless to say, these led to the large-scale destruction of natural resources. And yet the problems and hardships suffered by tribals were not acutely felt until the post-Independence period. This had been evident from the restrictions added in the New Forest Policy of 1952, which withdrew certain concessions that tribals had enjoyed during the colonial period. Further, there was now an emphasis on increasing the area under forest as well as on stringent regulation, policing and revenue earning. The policy also aimed to maintain one-third of the country's land area under forest. The enthusiasm to achieve the objective led to the claiming of even the treeless land as forest land to be brought under the control of the Forest Department. Through processes such as this, thousands of square kilometres of tribal land were brought under the Forest Department.

Interestingly, while on the one hand there was a concern to increase land under forest in the new policy, there was also an emphasis on the utilization of forest for national needs and maximization of revenue. National needs entailed the development of infrastructure, acceleration of industrial and agricultural growth and mineral exploitation. The private accumulation of profit by the Forest Department in collusion with contractors has been the other important factor. All these played havoc on existing forest resources. Paradoxically, most of the development projects in post-Independence India have taken place in tribal inhabited areas, which comprised a large tract of forest lands.

What is even more intriguing is that forest resources, despite being under state control and management, have undergone serious depletion through decades. In fact, in the thirty years since the declaration of policy in 1952, 4.3 million hectares of forest land was diverted to the non-forest purpose.[18] Thus, state control and management of forest resources have not improved the conservation of the forest. Rather, the process has been the reverse. Hence, in order to provide impetus to the protection and development of the forests, the Forest (Conservation) Act, 1980 was enacted. The Act forbids de-reservation of forest lands or use of forest lands for non-forest purposes or clearing of forest trees by state governments or other authorities without the prior approval of the Union government. The Act has proved to be instrumental in controlling the diversion of forest land for non-forest purposes. In fact, the rate of such diversion has fallen to a modest 16,500 hectares per year from the earlier figure of about 1.5 lakh hectares per year since the enactment of the Act.[19] The Act, however, had different implications for the tribals. In freezing legal use of land officially recorded as forests, the Act declared tribal forest dwellers as illegal occupants of their own lands. This led to a great deal of unrest among the tribal population. The Union Ministry of Environment and Forests issued several circulars which were either aimed at regularization of encroachers or resolution of disputed claims, but nothing tangible was achieved.

Forest Department statistics say that 23 per cent of India is forest land. But this is not a forested area. It simply means an area that is under the control of the Forest Department. The National Forest Policy of 1952 wanted to bring 33 per cent of land under forest cover. Between 1951 and 1988, the colonial Indian Forest Act (IFA), 1927 was used to enlarge the national forest estate by another 26 million hectares, that is, from 41 to 67 million hectares.[20] In the attempt to achieve this target, the Forest Department went on a spree to bring non-private land under its department through blanket notification, without even surveying their vegetation/ecological status or recognizing the rights of pre-existing occupants and users as required by law. Tribal areas, due to the poor recording of Adivasis customary rights, bore the brunt of this statistical achievement.

Does the onus of achieving ecological balance by maintaining 33 per cent of India's land under forest lie only with tribals? As it is, 60 per cent of state forests today are concentrated in 187 tribal districts which are confined to only one-third of the country. In the process, a large number of the most vulnerable tribes were disenfranchised of their customary resource rights without even their knowledge and labeled encroachers on their ancestral lands.[21] Tribals, thus, have contributed much more than their due share to the conservation of the forest wealth of India. The onus for maintaining ecological balance now lies with the rest of India for their contribution is negligible.

In the tribal-inhabited hill regions of the North-east, where shifting cultivation—seen as the bane of forest wealth—is an age-old practice, forest wealth is far more favourable than in the rest of India. Of course, land available for shifting cultivation has now shrunk because of various kinds of state and non-state-sponsored development activities. These have had a bearing on shifting cultivation since the cultivation cycle has now got reduced, which in turn has affected the fertility and productivity of the soil.

Notwithstanding that, their contribution to forest wealth far exceeds those of the rest of India. In fact, where state control and management of forest has been historically absent, there has been less destruction of forest wealth. The hill regions of the North-east—where state management of forest had limited entry with the forest policy of 1952—bear testimony to this. The total forested area in the region in the 1980s, including plains, constituted about 53 per cent of the total reported area. Of this, 36 per cent were reserved and 64 per cent were unclassified and were thus open for use by local people. If one was to exclude plains (plains had state control and management of forest since colonial rule, yet there has greater damage of forest wealth there), the area under forest in the region will further shoot up.[22] Equitable distribution of responsibility demands that non-tribal states and districts find out how much of their land is under forest cover and how much they have to contribute to maintaining the national standard.

Nature and Terms of Exchange

Several provisions have been made for the protection and welfare of the tribal people. Prominent among them are affirmative action programmes, on which crores of rupees have been spent by the government since Independence. The rest of the population sees tribals as one dependent solely on state patronage. Along with Dalits, they are seen as emptying the state exchequer. On close introspection, however, this is far from true. Justifications for development projects that displace millions from their homes and sources of livelihood have been made on the ground that the projects are going to be of immense benefit to the country, region or locality. The generation of power, extension of irrigation facilities and opportunities for employment, development of infrastructure, etc., are some of the reasons invoked in support of such projects. There is hardly any doubt that such projects bring about development and contribute to economic growth. The irony is that the benefits of such development have hardly accrued to people who have made possible these projects by their sacrifice.

Notwithstanding these developments, only 5 per cent of villages in Jharkhand were electrified and only 7.2 per cent of the total area was under irrigation by March 1973. Further, despite the rapid urbanization of tribal areas, the percentage of tribal people living in urban areas was hardly visible.[23] Since then, there has been further development in the state. By 1996 in Jharkhand, for example, eight major and fifty-five medium hydraulic projects along with many more minor projects had come up. Needless to say, these displaced a large number of households. Yet the area under irrigation in Jharkhand constituted only 7.68 per cent of the net sown area and households electrified were a mere 9.04 per cent. As many as 201 large- and medium-scale industries have come up in Jharkhand, displacing a large number of families on the one hand and providing employment to lakhs of people on the other.[24] Yet the benefits of these did not go to tribal people of Jharkhand or the displaced tribals. This can be vividly illustrated by citing the case of coal mine industries. Between 1981–85, the industry displaced 32,750 families, but provided a job to only 11,901 heads of households.[25] The gravity of this situation is compounded by the fact that the displaced, until recent years, were hardly thought to be rehabilitated. They received only cash compensation. Yet, even here the state has been found faltering in its responsibility. It was found out in 1988 that after thirty years of filling the Hirakud reservoir, compensation amounting to Rs 15 crore was due for payment to 9913 claimants who lost their land.[26] In the case of the Machkund hydro-electric project, only a few households enjoyed the benefits of being rehabilitated, while the benefits of the project in general were hardly received by the displaced. In terms of irrigation, electric power, tourism, pisciculture and other schemes for economic development, the government, for example, justified the Upper Kolab project. However, the displaced had none of these benefits.[27]

What has been the net result of the two kinds of interventions? One is that the gap between tribes and the rest of the population with respect to the fruits of development is widening. There is no doubt that there has been an increase in literacy rate, decrease in the size of people below the poverty line, decrease in the school dropout rate, etc. Still, the affirmative action programme to bridge the gap has not borne results. To illustrate, the gap between Scheduled Tribes and the general population in respect of literacy rate was 18.15 per cent in 1971, which increased to 19.88 per cent in 1981 and 22.61 per cent in 1991. People below the poverty line, with respect to the general rural population, stood at 53 per cent in 1977–78 and 37 per cent in 1993–94. The corresponding figure for Scheduled Tribes has been 72 per cent in 1977–78 and 52 per cent in 1993–94. By 2004–05, the share of the tribal population living below the poverty line declined to 46.5 per cent compared to 27.6 per cent for the population as a whole.[28] The share of agricultural labour among tribes has witnessed a phenomenal increase. Landlessness, too, has increased manifold. It is worth noting that it is unimaginable to think of tribes as landless, as land and forest have been traditionally their life support system. However, by 1993–94, as many as 48 per cent had begun to be enumerated as rural-labour households, which was much higher compared to 30 per cent for the non-tribal population. Further, the size of wage labour has been much higher in central India than in the North-eastern region. On average, nearly 50 per cent of households depended on wage employment in the central India belt, compared to only 17.30 per cent in the North-eastern states (Thorat 2006:184). Thus, although there has been a decline in people living below the poverty line, the level of poverty in the tribal population, especially in the central India region, is still much higher than the national average and the gap between the two continues to be one of the major issues of concern in poverty discourse in India. The poverty level and size, however, varies across regions, states and even tribes. The examples cited are merely illustrative, not exhaustive.

Much of the reason as to why the gap has remained intact—or even widening—is inherent in the way tribal problems have been articulated by the state and state apparatus. The tribal problem has primarily been couched in terms of social and economic backwardness arising from their geographical and social isolation. Hence the whole discourse on tribes has been around the question of integration through the extension of civil, political and social rights. Yet, the economic rights which tribes enjoyed—and which was their critical asset—have been usurped by the state in exchange for the above-mentioned rights. In fact, the extension of civil, political and social rights has become the arena of legitimizing the expropriation of resources of the tribal people.

In fact, the integration of tribes has been seen as the panacea of their problems. However, if one looks at the nature of integration, one finds that the relationship between tribes and non-tribes and even the state, has been overwhelmingly interspersed with exploitation, domination and discrimination, which is conveniently overlooked.

Tribal Heritage and People's Rights

Meenakshi Natarajan

The series of human progression is not yet completely known to us, but it is believed that the human race originated from Africa. Thereafter, through perpetual mobility, humans populated every nook and corner of the earth. Though there have been long migrations of human populations in prehistoric times from continent to continent, it is well established by genetics scientists that the people now recognized as aboriginals, indigenous or tribals are among those who have been residents in their habitats over a very long time.[1] The speciality of these communities is their innate intelligence and fundamentally natural lifestyle. In time, civilizations based on agriculture and domestication of animals flourished near rivers and in plains. Tribal communes have always lived in unity with nature, with notable deviation from these civilizations.

Tribal communities comprise up to 8 per cent of India's population and are spread across the country.[2] In North-eastern states, the Kukis, Nagas and Mundas are prime subsets of tribal communities. The eastern region has the Santhals and Halba subsets, whereas the western and central region have various subsets such as Gond, Baiga, Korku, Bheel, Sahariya and Bhilala. Each has their own beliefs, rituals, language, lifestyle and culture. The association of tribal communities with their soil and their innate lifestyle without greed is an essential lesson for all of humanity.

History

Tribal societies have, however, always struggled to retain their pride and freedom. They could never abide authoritarianism. They waged open war against colonial rule in many parts of the country. Battles were fought with imperialist rulers against torture and oppression of tribal communities and against taxation on forest plantations. The nineteenth century Santhal rebellion under the leadership of Birsa Munda and the martyrs Siddhu and Kanhu Murmu's struggle for tribal rights are well known. The fight against the British was initiated well before the 1857 revolution by central India's Gond leaders through the Bundela rebellion in 1842. Tantya Bheel, Bheema Nayak and Khajya Nayak created pandemonium in Jhabua and Nimad regions. Gond ruler Shankar Shah and Raghunath Shah came to be known as martyrs.

Within seven years of the formation of the Congress, in its eighth convention in Allahabad in 1892, under the chairmanship of W.C. Banerjee, the party appealed to the British government to look into problems arising from the Forest Act, 1884. In 1898 in Madras, under the chairmanship of Anand Mohan Bose, the fourteenth convention of the Congress put forward the idea that the aim of the forest law was not to hurt the indigenous people; the law was not for revenue collection, but forest conservation.[3]

Then, between 1921–24, several tribal groups participated in the Non-Cooperation Movement. On 9 March 1930, Seth Govind Das, Dwarka Prasad Mishra and Ravishankar Shukla met Mahatma Gandhi in Jambusar in Gujarat to organize the Jangal Satyagraha. At the time, Gandhiji was leading the Namak Satyagraha. He asked them to seek counsel from Jawaharlal Nehru. Due to Nehru's detention, the three leaders met Motilal Nehru and ran the andolan with his blessings. Das, Mishra, Shukla and D.K. Mehta were arrested. In Betul, Madhya Pradesh, under the leadership of Seth Deepchand Gothi, 5000 Gonds and Korkus broke the forest law. The revolution spread in districts of the old Central Provinces and Baraar. In Janjgir, Chhindwara, Dhamtari and Mandala in Madhya Pradesh and Chhattisgarh, Congress leaders fully supported and led the tribal groups to protest against the forest law and forest taxation. In central India and in various parts of today's Chhattisgarh, tribal groups were organized in large chunks for the satyagraha. The main aim of the Jangal Satyagraha was to stop the oppression of tribal groups under the forest law.

Question of Tribal Heritage and Rights

In 1931, census commissioner J.H. Hutton put forward the suggestion that to preserve the beliefs of tribal communities, self-governing reserved regions be demarcated for them. Well-known tribal activist and anthropologist Verrier Elwin, too, held a similar view. However, this thought faced harsh criticism too.

There have always been differing viewpoints regarding conservation of tribal lifestyle all around the world. The first belief is that tribals should be free, with a right to rule in their region. Outsiders should not have the right to interfere with their lifestyle. The counter belief is that they should be integrated into the mainstream.

Elwin, a proponent of the first line of thought, believed, 'Integration isn't possible without political and spiritual equality'.[4] He drew the attention of the nation state towards the need to conserve tribal privacy. He challenged and rejected the belief of imposing one's own thought on them.

Social worker Amritlal Vithaldas Thakkar, known popularly as Thakkar bapa, held the opposite view. Thakkar bapa had spent 35 years in service of tribals and fought for the rights of tribal people through the Indian Scheduled Tribe Organization and Bheel Seva Mandal, drawing inspiration from Congress leader Gopal Krishna

Gokhale. He led the way for the involvement of tribals in the nation-building task. It was Thakkar bapa who made Gandhi aware of the plight of the Adivasis. That was one reason why Gandhi asked young Elwin to take Thakkar bapa's help and move into an Adivasi village for work. Elwin followed Gandhi's advice and spent the rest of his life in remote tribal areas, bringing through his writings knowledge about Adivasi culture and society to the rest of the world. These interactions helped build bridges between the national freedom movement and Adivasi communities.

However, the imposition of one's own belief on tribals invariably started in the name of including them in the mainstream. This raises the question, what defines the mainstream? Does wearing shirt-pants and speaking English or doing *yagna* symbolize joining the mainstream? Which god, mode of worship or rituals of marriage, birth and death would be considered mainstream? Should the strong opponents—from the Sangh Parivar—of conversion of tribals to Christianity not look at their own deeds? On the one hand, they oppose the conversion of tribals to Christianity and then impose their own rituals on them. Should everyone not have the right to live their lives in their own way?

Jaipal Singh Munda, a member of the Constituent Assembly, had said, 'You can't teach democracy to tribals. You need to learn democratic values from them. They are the most democratic community on earth'.[5] Through his adept mode of reasoning, he sought to emphasize that tribal lifestyle is the first school of democracy that ought to provide democratic inspiration to other classes of society. We do not have any right to impose our beliefs and values on them.

India's first Prime Minister Jawaharlal Nehru vehemently rejected both points of view. He said: 'Conservative settlements and imposing beliefs to the lifestyle of tribal communities in guise of adding tribals to mainstream.'[6] In the Constituent Assembly, when Jaipal Munda raised the issue of tribal rights and oppression done to them over thousands of years, Nehru pointed out to him that tribal rights, justice and equality were concerns that the Constitution would take into cognizance. His ideology is explained by only one word used on a different occasion. When he was asked what the stance towards tribal groups should be, he said, 'Humility'.[7] This is the soul and purview of the provisions towards tribal heritage in the Constitution drafted by Dr B.R. Ambedkar.

When we think with humility, only then can we do justice with tribal communities. We will neither consider their beliefs inferior nor impose our rituals and beliefs. This is Nehru's suggested third way. The 'panchsheel' way given by Nehru is the foundation of equal rights and justice for tribal communities.[8] According to it:

1. **Tribal people have the right to live according to their innate conscience. There should be no imposition of any external values on them. They should promote their art, culture and tradition.**

   This is an important thought. The opposite has been happening either through 'ghar wapsis' organized by Sewa Bharti organizations in the name of culture or through missionary institutions who use the notion of making them civilized.[9] It is wrong to force spiritual slavery either by offering humanitarian services like education and health or luring them with these basic necessities. Each individual or community has the liberty to choose any religious view according to their own intelligence. It may be either Buddhism, Jainism, Christianity, Sikhism, Shaiva, Vaishnava, Kabir Panth or any other way. The Constitution considers tribal lifestyle as an invaluable heritage. It prohibits any external interference and respects the privacy of individuals.

2. **The rights to land and forest of tribal groups must be respected.**

   Tribal innate consciousness has established an interrelationship with nature over centuries. The Constitution recognizes this compassionate identification specifically. On use of land for development purposes, their consent is required. It also understands the share of their innate intelligence in natural resource management and its compulsion.

3. **We should educate and skill tribal people for administration and development of their regions.**
   External influence in matters concerning them should be minimal. On the socio-economic front, marginalized tribal groups can be truly developed with their own contribution, otherwise the development would be hollow. The Constitution ensures their role in nation building through reservation in education and administrative fields. Their wholesome development has been institutionalized.

4. **Work should be done through their cultural institutions rather than building a hyper-administrative framework.**
   Any confrontation must be avoided. In a society, true policy can be made through integrating the voice of wisdom gained through their experience of ages and their innate intelligence. Through reservation, the Constitution ensures the oasis of their accumulated intelligence in the Lok Sabha, Vidhan Sabha, Panchayat and urban local body elections. Community leadership is accepted through the PESA. Scheduled regions are granted special status. The responsibility is ensured by constituting advisory committees in transparent mode.

5. **We should evaluate our results not through capitalist and statistical calculations, but through the quality of pure humanistic standards.**
   The Constitution frees them from discrimination and oppression. It guarantees social and economic empowerment

for all oppressed and marginalized sections, including Adivasis, of Indian society.

This would pave the way for an end to the oppression of tribal communities and help them attain socio-politico-economic equality, justice and proper rights. The Constitution's Fifth and Sixth Schedules grant special provision for states and districts that have tribal groups in majority. Every state Governor has the authority to evaluate and publish an annual report on the social, economic and political situation of tribal groups and to establish a committee to resolve issues between tribal groups. The intention behind this arrangement was that if the ruling government proved insensitive or callous about issues related to tribal people, the Governor, free from any political affiliation, would be well placed to keep an eye on their condition. Large populations of tribal groups reside in regions with an abundance of natural minerals and water sources. On the one hand it is necessary to use minerals and build dams for electricity and irrigation purposes and work towards the conservation of forests and wildlife for national interest. On the other hand, one cannot overlook the pain inflicted through displacement of tribals from their land for the building of dams or through deforestation or for mining.

It is our collective responsibility to keep tribal land free from land, forest and alcohol mafia and illegal mining. The panchsheel way is the first step in this direction and the foundation stone of tribal people's freedom. Indira Gandhi, too, was compassionate towards the tribal community. She laid the foundation of the tribal sub-plan, a policy to present tribal regions with better opportunities and structures in the fields of education and health. Co-operative committees were formed for small forest products to keep middlemen away. Due to the policy, non-tribal people could not own land in scheduled regions. As per its vision, tribal hostels were established throughout districts and grants and scholarship for higher education and research purposes were ensured.

The 1994 Bhuria Committee was formed to look into tribal welfare and rights. For better co-operation and participation of Scheduled Tribes in politics and to ensure the rights of their community, the committee put forward the proposal of including panchayats and urban local bodies in tribal regions. For a long time, retired bureaucrat B.D. Sharma had fought for a traditional political system for tribal people. This committee gave shape to that idea. The PESA law for the spread of panchayats into tribal regions was recommended by this committee. However, till date, many states haven't implemented PESA. The Municipalities Extension to Scheduled Areas (MESA) law for expanding urban local bodies was not even passed by Parliament. A detailed study by the United Nations Development Programme (UNDP) records that barring Rajasthan, Kerala, Maharashtra and Haryana, most other states have defaulted on the full implementation of PESA provisions.[10]

However, in 2006, in a historic announcement, the UPA government gave tribal communities the right to lease forests. The determination criteria of eligibility for the lease was left to Gram Sabhas. It also decided on a minimum support price for small forest products.

Challenges

Despite many efforts of the administration, tribal communities lag behind in areas of education, health, employment and life expectancy. The literacy rate of the tribal community is a mere 59 per cent, when the national literacy rate is 73 per cent.[11] Despite having the constitutional right to study in their mother tongue, lack of execution of the policy and lack of good teachers leads to dropouts from schools.[12]

Dropout Rates in School Education for Scheduled Tribe Students

Year	Classes I–V			Classes I–VIII			Classes I–X		
	Boys	Girls	Total	Boys	Girls	Total	Boys	Girls	Total
2011-12	4.43	5.35	7.35	7.15	7.26	4.46	7.66	5.92	6.13
2012-13	3.12	3.23	5.06	4.75	4.9	2.63	2.62	2.62	3.33
2013-14	9.30	7. 31	3.49	8.46	4.48	2.63	2.61	4.62	3.1

(Source: Educational Statistics at a Glance, Department of School Education, Ministry of Education, formerly Ministry of Human Resource Development)

In my own experience, in Dindori district of Madhya Pradesh's Shahpura region, tribal students were unwillingly taught Sanskrit. They can't keep up in education because the medium of study isn't their mother tongue.

Life expectancy for tribal people is only 43 years. The child death rate is 8.3 per cent. Almost 40 per cent of tribal kids are malnourished.[13] According to the 2011 census, more than 43 per cent of the tribal population was below poverty line. Tribal communities don't have access to community rights. Talk of water, forest and land rights seem farfetched. They have to face the biased colonial mindset of forest officers. They are kept away from using even natural resources. They have to seek many permissions and no-objection letters even for a small fish or poultry business. Forest officers blame tribal communities for forest degradation. They do not understand that afforestation and forest management can't happen naturally without cooperation from tribal communities. In the Forest (Conservation) Act, 1980, forest officers have undue rights and tribal people have no rights. There has been a long-standing conflict and contestation between the Forest Department and Adivasi communities with respect to rights over forest land and forest produce. The law has remained heavily biased in favour of the Forest Department, depriving Adivasis of their traditional access and ownership of forest produce in the process.

Profit from mining in tribal regions has been kept away from tribal communities. Justice is often denied to tribal communities where the question of displacement caused by development-related large projects is concerned.

Degradation of forests due to large dams and mining is conveniently ignored by the system run by capitalist and corporate institutions. It is almost always that Scheduled Tribes face interference. Despite being only 8 per cent of the total population, they form 55 per cent of the displaced communities.[14]

Due to PESA and the Panchayati Raj Act, it is not possible to own their land without permission from Gram Sabhas. But interference has increased by constituting fake Gram Sabhas in tribal regions.[15] There have been various litigations involving the rights of communities as against those of the state; the petitions were clubbed together and brought under a case that is now known as 'Samata versus State'.[16] In this, the Supreme Court had ruled that no court can invalidate the legislated proposals of Gram Sabhas. But it has been observed that various states set up their own companies, with exemption given to them from all land ownership related acts and in turn, it is these companies that give lease to the land under their command to private companies, flouting the spirit of the land acquisition laws.[17] In such scenarios, tribal rights of water, forest and land are just on paper. Where 25 per cent of the nation's villages have the right to use forest for communities, only 3 per cent of forest land is yet validated. For exercising the CFR, the Forest Department and the village panchayat are jointly required to validate forest land over which community rights can be exercised. This validation of specific land sites has so far remained just about 3 per cent of the total land area that was expected to be brought under the CFR. There are only a few cases where justice is done fully to Adivasi communities with regard to their forest rights. Recently in Odisha, the Vedanta group wanted to mine the sacred mountain of the Niyamgiris, disrespecting their religious sentiments. The Supreme Court stopped the mining.

Inequality is apparent in tribal areas even today. On the one hand, there are people who gain billions from mining and on the other hand, tribal communities are victims of poverty and oppression. Mining is necessary for national development, but it should be done by sharing profits with tribal communities and seeking their active participation with compassion. These tribal regions are becoming centres of violent Left unity because of this inequality. Since the administration uses force to counter such action, these regions are being converted into armed camps and tribal communities are being torn between them. If the report to be made by governors annually is done so with dedication, this injustice to tribal communities may stop. But this is not happening.

Lack of education has also led to lack of opportunities. There hasn't been any vice chancellor (VC) or judge from the tribal community in our country. It was only recently that Sonajharia Minz was appointed as VC of the Sido Kanhu Murmu University in Jharkhand, the first instance of its kind since Independence.

Many reserved government posts remain vacant.[18]

Promise of Future

In my extensive work with Adivasi communities in India, I have noticed how these communities have a strong resentment against their exclusion from the development process and also due to large development projects. If I were to sum up their feelings, the following collective demands would be most appropriate:

1. We believe that the Indian government must identify the innate intelligence of tribal people and should come in agreement with them on moral, social, economic and political fronts. It should avoid the cultural terrorism of bringing their lifestyle to the mainstream. Their rituals and lifestyles must be identified in a different civil code.

The elected committee of tribal people must be institutionalized and through them, all the decisions involving tribal people must be taken. The provisions of PESA should be made mandatory and the advice by the Advisory Committees mandated by the Act must be fully acted upon.

2. The lease for community forest rights must be distributed. It should ensure an important place for Gram Sabhas in affairs of forest preservation.
3. The Gram Sabha should be conferred the right to prevent trafficking of tribal women and children.
4. A commission should be formed for the socio-economic rights of nomadic communities by identifying their population. Another advisory committee that takes policy decisions should be formed.

This would integrate tribal communities and calls for justice for tribal communities would stop. They would then get harmonious swaraj in true terms.

The Question of Integration

Kantilal Bhuria and Vikrant Bhuria

Introduction

Historically, Adivasis and Other Traditional Forest Dwellers (OTFDs) are known to have taken care of the forests that form the very basis of their livelihood. The symbiotic relation between such communities and the forests in which they lived was severely disrupted by legislations brought in by the colonial government. Besides, the sovereignty of the communities in relation to their environment was brought under a new regime in which the state became the dominating player. The colonial arrangement developed a view of forest dwellers as encroachers or potentially so, with an adversarial relation between the state and the forest-dwellers becoming the order of the day. To redress this myopic perspective, in 1959, Pandit Jawaharlal Nehru in his foreword to Verrier Elwin's *A Philosophy for NEFA*, proposed a policy on tribal development: Panchsheel, the 'Five Pillars of Tribal Development'. He emphasized the importance of integration of Adivasis without the dilution of their culture and way of life. Despite efforts to implement these principles, the difference between policy and implementation is enormous. While laws and policies are in place

to ensure good governance in tribal areas, institutions and Forest
Departments continue to undermine these provisions. Due to the
abundance of rich mineral resources, lands owned and occupied
by tribals have attracted commercial interests. While legitimate
for developmental reasons, these have led to the marginalization
of tribal voices and loss of autonomy and land. Adivasis have to
contend with ever-increasing threats from private interests such as
illegal mining, deforestation and encroachment by businesses and
government officials, which jeopardizes both the tribal way of life
and the environment.

The exploitation and displacement endured over the years
have given rise to a mistrust, which characterizes the relationship
between the state and the Adivasis today. Although attempts have
been made to assimilate Adivasis with the rest of the country over
the last 70 years, the historical differences between them and the
rest of society have never been greater in the last five years.

Problematizing the Adivasi

It must be emphasized that conceptually, 'Tribes', 'Tribal' and
'Adivasi' are only very recent classifications as a direct result of
colonialism. The 85 million Indians who are classified as Scheduled
Tribes[1] are diverse and heterogeneous—culturally, socially,
economically and politically—and spread over about 15 per cent of
the country's plains, forests and hills. For administrative convenience,
the colonial administration had deliberately categorized diverse
groupings in India on three lines, namely religion, caste and
tribe. Any peoples, from the hills, forests and frontiers who were
different from 'mainstream' society, did not follow 'mainstream'
religions such as Hinduism and Islam and did not fit into pervasive
class and caste permutations were automatically classified as Tribes
in the colonial paradigm. They were caricatured as primordial,
pre-political and pre-modern, in need of 'civilizing', which only
colonial rule could guarantee. Anything the colonial administration

did in tribal areas was automatically deemed to be necessary and developmental because of the Adivasi communities' supposed 'backwardness'.

Similarly, the colonial administration's Permanent Settlement (1793)[2], the Ryotwari settlement[3] and the India Forest Acts (1865 and 1878)[4] gave primacy to a pattern of land use distinctly titled towards settled agrarian communities. Specifically, land became property only through the exercise of human labour on it. This put Adivasis at a disadvantage because they were not settled cultivators. In fact, most Adivasis simply inhabited land, sometimes even sacralizing it. Land was never purely utilized either as a property or resource. The colonial administration consequently tried very hard to 'sedentarize' tribal communities, partly to streamline resource extraction and partly to extend the 'framework of governmentality'[5].

This stunted reading of social, economic and political realities created a host of mythologies and prejudices with respect to Adivasis and tribes in India. They were perceived to be isolated, self-sufficient, animist, underdeveloped and backward. Seemingly harmless, these mythologies have had serious policy and political implications. For example, tribes are seen as interlinked with castes in India, by policymakers, academics and even in popular perception. At one level, it is perhaps necessary to denote common subalternity, so as to emphasize the state's obligation to their upliftment and empowerment. However, this manufactured equivalence glosses over the fact that while the Dalit question is relatively centre stage in the nation's consciousness, the Adivasi question is not.

The issues, needs and aspirations of Adivasis are completely different from Dalits. Yet, their issues have not been adequately studied or addressed separately with the seriousness they require. Just to cite one prominent example, representation looms large in the Dalit imagination and hence shapes Dalit politics and economy. In stark contrast, autonomy looms large in the Adivasi imagination. In fact, Yudhisthir Mishra, a Constituent Assembly (CA) member from Odisha, received memorandums from Adivasi communities which questioned the CA's representativeness. They did not believe the CA represented them and emphasized their right to govern themselves[6]. Clearly, even then, autonomy was infinitely more important than self-representation to Adivasis.

It is therefore no surprise that at the same time, Adivasi communities in Jharkhand and Nagaland were demanding autonomy within India. These sentiments were also echoed in the CA, where P.R. Thakur from Bengal argued[7] that tribes were a 'unique political minority' who adhered to evolved practices of self-government. Carrying the argument further, Jaipal Singh, another member in the CA, argued that tribal modes of self-government could serve as a lesson to India's deeply hierarchical caste society. In fact, Singh went so far as to argue that states should not be organized along linguistic lines (which is what happened eventually), but as self-governing units, adopting from tribal governance systems.

However, these arguments did not carry the day in the CA. Occupied with the task of integrating the various peoples and regions of the Subcontinent into a nation-state, India's founders were more concerned with the project of national integration. For example, Lakshmi Narayan Sahu, a CA member from Odisha, strongly argued against permitting tribal forms of self-government as this could enable frontier tribes to merge with tribes across India's frontiers, primarily in areas like Tibet or Burma[8].

In fact, even though Dr B.R. Ambedkar argued[9] that '(t)he Aboriginal Tribes have not yet developed any political sense' and could therefore 'disturb the balance' between minority and majority constituencies 'without doing any good to themselves' by claiming self-representation, Adivasis were extended reservations by the collective wisdom of the CA.

However, there has always been tension between the mainstream notion of democracy as representation and the Adivasi notion of democracy as autonomy. For the state, democracy essentially means a uniform and centralized administrative and political infrastructure. The Adivasi peoples have not been able to effectively participate in this system of representation for various reasons ranging from geographical isolation, diversity and identity, just to name a few. They have also not been able to unite as a strong political bloc. Consequently, their politics has centred on demanding greater autonomy, both to undo the social and economic disadvantage they face and re-shape their lives as per their respective aspirations. This means halting the displacement they have faced because of 'the pressures and imperatives of development'[10]. It is noteworthy that an Adivasi is five times as likely to be displaced as a non-Adivasi for development projects[11]. It is estimated that since Independence, about twenty million Adivasis have been displaced [12]. Numerous Adivasi movements— such as the Jharkhand movement, the Bhoomi Sena, the Kashtakari Sanghatana or the militant Left movements—have demanded autonomy, arguing that they are culturally distinct.

Precisely because of these thorny issues, numerous government initiatives in the last seventy years have tried to balance the twin objections of national integration and autonomy on the one hand and ensure that the needs and aspirations of numerous Adivasi peoples are sensitively addressed. For example, the 1959 high-powered committee—chaired by the former president of the All India Congress Committee, U.N. Dhebar—found that the rapid industrialization that India had undertaken post-Independence would 'sweep (the Adivasis) off their feet' and that Adivasis strongly felt 'that all arguments in favour of preservation and development of forests are intended to refuse them their demands'. It argued that 'we have to see that the foundations of tribal life are not shaken and the house does not crash'[13]. This was reiterated by other official reports[14] in the 1980s, which pointed out that 'the tribal people are at a critical point in their history . . .' since they were 'losing command over resources at a very fast rate but are also facing social disorganization which is unprecedented in their history'. These reports went on to indict the state since it '. . . sometimes tends to adopt a partisan role and become a privy even for actions not quite legal simply because the matter concerns voiceless small communities'.

And therein lies the rub. India's developmental impulses have pitted it against the Adivasis in more ways than one. They face multiple levels of oppression from the forest bureaucracy that treats and penalizes them as encroachers. Like in colonial times, private corporations see Adivasis as impediments in accessing natural resources. These corporations pressurize local administration and state governments to expedite 'development projects'. The sad reality is that Adivasis haven't ever been partners in economic development; it marginalizes them further. And because Adivasis have not been able to establish themselves as a powerful interest group, their legitimate claims and grievances are restricted to the districts in which they live. Their voices are rarely heard in the corridors of power in either the national or state capitals.

To rectify these anomalies, a radical set of statutes and policies were spearheaded by the Union government which were eventually hailed the world over as the rights-based paradigm. These were based on the understanding that the state must consistently expand people's capabilities (their real freedoms) and opportunities to achieve states of being that they value[15]. In the case of Adivasis, this meant extending a greater degree of autonomy within the constitutional framework, without compromising the integrity of the nation-state, to deepen the foundations of India's status as an effective and legitimate democracy. After all, every government is mandated to uphold the constitutional values of liberty, equality and fraternity, especially to secure a life of dignity and security for the 10.42 crore[16] Adivasis and OTFDs.

Consequently, the PESA[17] formally acknowledged the right of Adivasis in Schedule V areas to self-governance. For the first time, the PESA prioritized the Adivasi Gram Sabha's right to make decisions on a host of governance issues, including land acquisition, mining for minor minerals, ownership of minor forest produce, etc. The PESA tried to reimagine democracy as more deliberative, decentralized and autonomous within the existing politico-administrative framework.

Building on this framework, the 2006 FRA[18] gave statutory recognition to the unrecognized but customary rights of Adivasis and OTFDs. The FRA recognized their rights to land as well as non-timber forest produce and the community right of control and management which was hitherto under the Forest Department. It introduced a new category of forests, Community Forest Resources (CFRs), which includes all types of forest lands, including Reserve Forests and Protected Forests notified under the Indian Forest Act (IFA). This empowered the communities to conserve and manage forests. 'The FRA formalized the historical and traditional rights of Adivasis. Re-instating them as custodians of forests, it recognized their rights to live in the forest, to self-cultivate, to own and use minor forest produce and to have a host of community/customary rights. Perhaps most radically, it made Gram Sabhas central to forest governance . . . If properly implemented, the FRA can dramatically enhance the lives of Adivasis in 1.77 lakh villages and lead to the conservation of at least 40 million hectares of forests!'[19]

Similarly, the 2013 Right to Fair Compensation and Transparency in Land Acquisition, Rehabilitation and Resettlement (LARR) Act[20] replaced the Land Acquisition Act, 1894. Apart from enhancing compensation for displaced people and providing for commensurate rehabilitation and resettlement, the LARR Act mandated that any development project seeking to acquire Adivasi land would have to seek prior and informed consent of the Gram Sabha. It also necessitated that the consent of at least 70 per cent of the affected people would have to be sought if the land was being acquired by a private firm or a public-private project.

These seemingly disconnected statues were designed to collectively address the Adivasi aspiration for greater autonomy. It is strongly felt by these communities that there is 'disregard for their values and culture, breach of protective legislations, serious material and social deprivation, and aggressive resource alienation. To redress this, the changes recommended to the laws, regulations and rules strived to protect Adivasi communities from land alienation and to ensure that their rights over resources are handed back and protected'.[21]

Status of Adivasis in the Last Few Years

Despite the progress made in the past two decades, the National Democratic Alliance (NDA) government is systematically withdrawing from the progress India has made in better integrating Adivasis socially, economically and politically. Since 2014, it has reoriented the state to withdraw from its core responsibilities: that of uplifting and empowering Adivasis. Even though the ruling dispensation and the Rashtriya Swayamsevak Sangh's Vanvasi Kalyan Ashram[22] have claimed to uphold Adivasi rights, they have spearheaded numerous anti-Adivasi policies. Since the NDA came to power, alienation of tribal land has increased significantly. This alienation has been facilitated by systematically diluting the statutory protections that guarantee rights to Adivasis. Adivasi lands have been subjected to 'developmental terrorism' by diverting them to large corporations for projects such as mining.

For example, the UPA government had formed the high-level Xaxa Committee to study the situation. Its report brought out the nuances of the situation in a well-studied manner. However later, the NDA government chose not to act on the Xaxa Committee report.

Furthermore, amendments to the Land Acquisition and Rehabilitation Act and the Mines and Minerals (Development and Regulation) Act (MMDRA)[23] by the BJP government at the Centre and numerous state governments have allowed private companies to acquire Adivasi and forest land without the free and informed consent of Gram Sabhas. This has led to an accelerated diversion of forest and Adivasi lands for commercial projects as witnessed in Odisha, Chhattisgarh and Jharkhand.[24] Equally shockingly, the NDA has removed the provision of compensation, rehabilitation and resettlement of Adivasis from the MMDRA Act. The 2015 MMDRA Amendment Act also allowed for exceptions to some mining licences to be given prior to obtaining clearances mandated by the FRA.[25] This has led to the wholesale marginalization of Scheduled Tribes.

Similarly, in 2017, Prime Minister Modi announced[26] that all kinds of individual and collective claims under the Forest Rights Act would be settled within two months. The bitter reality is that only 20-25 per cent of claims have been actually settled till date.[27] Adivasi communities are being systematically denied their traditional rights using legal loopholes, with many such cases in Odisha, Chhattisgarh, Jharkhand and Maharashtra, where the state governments have routinely watered down the provisions of the FRA to divert forest land for mining purposes. The period between 2014 and 2018 shows the slowest execution of the FRA since its inception. According to reports of the Ministry of Tribal Affairs, government authorities have rejected more than 43 per cent claims filed by forest dwellers across India.[28] Further, some states have illegally diluted Community Forest Resource rights by handing over CFR rights to the Joint Forest Management Committee or the Forest Revenue Department.[29]

These amendments have directly contributed to undermining Adivasi aspirations for greater autonomy and agency over determining their own lives. Exacerbating this, by establishing the National Tribal Advisory Council under the chairmanship of the Prime Minister in 2015,[30] the NDA has blatantly and illegally usurped the powers of the Governors, the National Commission for Scheduled Tribes (NCST), the Ministry of Tribal Affairs and Tribal Advisory Councils in the states. This has not only destroyed federal and democratic principles, but also led to the accelerated diversion of forest and Adivasi land for myopic commercial projects.

Adding salt to injury, the NDA's proposed amendments to the Indian Forest Act[31] included 'giving forest officials the power to shoot Adivasis without any liability, allowing forest officials to withdraw Adivasi rights without cause and to forcefully relocate them against their will'.[32] The amendments were both illegal and morally unconscionable and completely negated the idea of democratic governance of forests. Although this bill was withdrawn after widespread protests and pressure,[33] the intention of this government has been to centralize power, not decentralize it. This impulse contravenes any kind of autonomy to the Adivasis and OTFDs, which further makes their integration into mainstream India that much more difficult.

Similarly in 2017, the NDA's National Tiger Conservation Authority[34] issued an order barring recognition of forest rights in tiger reserves, affecting lakhs of Adivasi and OTFDs. Subsequently, the NDA stopped intervening in the Supreme Court, where the Forest Rights Act was being challenged. This is despite the fact that it is the government's duty to uphold Adivasi rights and work towards their welfare. The NDA government at the Centre did not send any counsel for four hearings when petitioners were seeking to evict millions of Adivasis. Consequently, on 13 February 2019, a Supreme Court order threatened to evict more than one million Adivasis and other forest dwellers.[35] This was based on the fallacious understanding that Adivasis and OTFDs threaten the very ecosystem they inhabit. This glaring deficit in understanding ground realities ignores the fact that these communities are central to protecting and preserving fragile ecosystems that are under threat from indiscriminate deforestation, poaching and myopic commercial ventures.

Exacerbating the situation, the NDA enacted the Compensatory Afforestation Fund (Management and Planning Authority) Act (CAMPA)[36] purportedly to promote 'afforestation'. There was widespread objection from Adivasi rights groups because they rightly felt that CAMPA subjugated Adivasis and sabotaged their rights. Not only does CAMPA create an ecological imbalance by promoting monoculture afforestation which destroys the rich variety of flora and fauna, but also adversely affects the livelihoods and food security of Adivasis and OTFDs which form a vital source of nutritional security. Furthermore, Gram Sabhas have no voice in the management of the compensatory funds that any commercial venture has to deposit for any development on Adivasi/forest land. CAMPA directly violates the democratic structure of forest governance laid down in the FRA—under Section 3(1)(i) and Section (5) which mandate that Gram Sabhas control and manage all aspects of forest management, including financial resources—by usurping fiscal powers meant for Gram Sabhas for itself and the forest officialdom.

The NDA has also overseen the systematic dilution of all those policies that were designed to uplift and empower Adivasis.[37] For example, the Tribal Sub-Plan or TSP (renamed Scheduled Tribe Component) expenditure dropped from Rs 32,387 crore (2014–15) to Rs 20,000 crore (2015–16) and then increased to Rs 24,005 crore (2016–17). Even though it subsequently further increased to Rs 31,920 crore (2017–18), the NDA has added non-targeted generic/administrative expenditure (such as grants towards infrastructure maintenance, farm loan waivers, Good Governance Fund, Sports Authority of India, etc.,) as Adivasi welfare to inflate figures. If these are excluded, the NDA has slashed funds for Adivasi welfare by almost 52 per cent (compared to 2014–15[38])!

The apathy of the government is also reflected in the manner in which the roster system in universities was diluted.[39] The government waited one year before bringing in an ordinance just before the 2019 general elections to address this issue. Dr Ambedkar had started the Post-Matric Scholarship in 1945 to uplift and empower the Scheduled Castes and Scheduled Tribes. Yet the Modi government withheld Rs 2871 crore of the scholarship from 2014–16.[40] Consequently, lakhs of Adivasis have been denied financial support.

Similarly, the state's apathy towards the welfare of Adivasis also extended to MGNREGA, which made a significant difference to lives of Adivasis. In the UPA's last year of government, eighteen lakh SC and ST households completed the full 100 days of work.[41] Under the NDA, wage increases have been a paltry 2.7 per cent in 2017–18 compared to 9 per cent per annum during the UPA tenure.[42] Furthermore, wage payments worth Rs 9,179 crore have been defaulted by the NDA government in 2016–17 and state officials were reportedly coerced through informal channels (WhatsApp groups) to deny work under the programme,[43] undermining its demand-driven nature. Consequently, the person days generated under the scheme also declined from 257 crore in 2010–11 to 166 crore in 2014–15 and to 167 crore in 2016–17.[44]

Insidious Danger to Adivasi Empowerment

Perhaps the biggest danger to the Adivasi quest for self-determination comes from the Akhil Bharatiya Vanvasi Kalyan Ashram (ABVKA), which claims to have about 20,000 projects in 52,000 villages.[45] In January 2018, the sarsanghchalak of the RSS urged its workers to 'embrace' the weaker sections of society 'including tribal communities and Dalits'. The RSS does not acknowledge the autonomous identities of Adivasi communities. To them, even the name Adivasis (literally: first inhabitants) is problematic since that would denote that they are distinct from the fourfold Hindu varna fold. The preferred term for Adivasis that the RSS and the ABVKA use is *vanvasis* (the forest-dwellers). The underlying principle of this argument is that Adivasis are essentially Hindus who have strayed from the Hindu path and need to be 'mainstreamed' back into the Hindu fold.[46] This is in pursuance of their larger project of realizing a Hindu *rashtra*.

Consequently, much of the ABVKA's work is geared towards Hinduizing Adivasis and countering the 'dangers' of Christianity and Islam. As an RSS publication titled 'RSS: Widening Horizons' argues, 'the systematic alienation of the tribals . . . who form an inseparable part of the Hindu society through proselytization . . . demanded immediate corrective measures . . . They had all along been a most exploited lot and an easy prey for unscrupulous conversion by Christian missionaries. It is to counter this twin menace of British legacy, that the Bharateeya Vanavasi Kalyan Ashram was founded.'[47]

The ABVKA does this by instrumentally adopting *seva* (service) to convince Adivasis to stay in the Hindu fold, and systematically influencing Adivasi children against Christians and Muslims. For example, Sewa Bharati (an ABVKA associate) boasted that 'to cultivate faith in our religion in the minds of Tribals, Sewa Bharati has . . . sent (Adivasi children) to Ayodhya to undergo training in 'Shri Ram Katha Pravachan' (discourses of Ramayana). This training lasted 8 months under the guidance of special Saints and Mahatmas. Now . . . they will live in the villages and propagate Ram Katha.'[48] In itself, religious worship seems innocuous. However, this religio-ideological training may lead to communalism among the Adivasis.

But what is equally worrying is that the NDA government has slashed state support for Adivasi welfare programmes, perhaps knowing full well that the ABVKA is well placed to fill the vacuum. This not only undermines the state but has dangerous ramifications for India's social contract.

Way Forward

Mahatma Gandhi famously argued[49]: 'I will give you a talisman. Whenever you are in doubt, or when the self becomes too much with you, apply the following test. Recall the face of the poorest and the weakest man whom you may have seen and ask yourself if the step you contemplate is going to be of any use to him. Will he gain anything by it? Will it restore him to a control over his own life and destiny? In other words, will it lead to swaraj for the hungry and spiritually starving millions? Then you will find your doubts and yourself melting away.' In this light, the state has to consistently strive to extend the promise of the nation. Economic growth has to be accompanied by tangible programmes to extend values of liberty, equity and fraternity. The FRA, PESA, LARR and MMRA Acts strived to further this agenda and to make each Adivasi an equal partner in the nation's growth. Despite the many reverses made, it is important to extend and enhance the rights and freedoms that were guaranteed to Adivasis. In this context, the following ideas need to be seriously considered[50]:

Revisiting role of Governors: By and large, Governors do not adequately exercise their constitutional power towards the protection and welfare of the tribal communities. To ensure this is done properly, the actions taken by the Governor for furthering the interests of tribal communities should be clearly mentioned in the annual Governor's Reports submitted to the President. A special Governor's Cell for Scheduled Tribes (as has already been initiated in some states) should be instituted to assist the Governor effectively. It should comprise tribal scholars and professionals from a wide range of fields.

Reimagining the Tribes Advisory Councils (TACs): TACs are an integral part of the administrative structure of the Fifth Schedule. Because of its potential, it needs to be dramatically restructured:

1. Currently, the TAC consists of 20 members of which two-thirds are comprised elected MLAs belonging to the Scheduled Tribes. The rest are nominated members who generally tend to be government officials working in ministries and departments associated with tribal development. The composition of the TAC needs to be dramatically restructured. The number of MLAs should be restricted to half the members of the TAC. Furthermore, these elected representatives must come from different political parties, rather than only from the ruling

party. The remaining half should comprise chairpersons of the district Panchayat bodies (or chairpersons of the Autonomous Council, wherever established) of the Scheduled Areas.

2. Constitutional provisions, laws, policies and administrative matters pertaining to the Scheduled Tribes must come under its ambit. Similarly, the tribal development plan of a state and its outlay should be approved by the TAC before it is sent to the Legislative Assembly. In the same vein, the Tribal Welfare Department should be made accountable to the TAC. It should present its annual plan, budget and performance report to the TAC and receive its approval for the next year.

Enhancing Self-Governance: The provisions of the Sixth Schedule provide considerable space for self-governance. For example, through the Autonomous Councils in Meghalaya, Mizoram, Tripura and Assam, tribes of the North-east have been able to protect their habitat, land, forests, natural resources, culture and identity. This is because they have the power to enact legislations and execute schemes on their own. In stark contrast, tribes in the mainland have fared miserably in all these spheres. There is an urgent need for extending the pattern of the Sixth Schedule in the form of Autonomous Councils in the Fifth Schedule areas as has been provided for in the provisions of the PESA 1996. The specific provision notes that 'the State Legislature shall endeavour to follow the pattern of the Sixth Schedule to the Constitution while designing the administrative arrangements in the Panchayats at district levels in the Scheduled Areas'. This pattern would provide tribal areas with an institutional structure that mediates between the state government and hamlet-level Gram Sabha.

Revisiting Functioning of NCST: The primary objective of the NCST is to safeguard the rights of Adivasi communities over mineral resources and water resources, improve the efficacy of relief and rehabilitation measures and reduce and ultimately eliminate the practice of shifting cultivation that leads to their continuous disempowerment and degradation of land. The NCST's role also includes inquiring, monitoring and following up on proper compensation or to suggest framing a special investigation team (SIT) in certain cases. However, as things stand today, the Commission is toothless and consistently ignored by the government. It cannot look into law-and-order matters. It has been reduced to playing an advisory role, defeating the very purpose for which it was formed.

The Commission is supposed to investigate cases by constituting a team at its headquarters in Delhi or through its regional offices in Bhopal, Raipur, Bhubaneswar, Ranchi, Jaipur and Shillong. Only the Chairperson, Secretary, Assistant Director, Research Officer and Section Officer can be entrusted with the investigation. The Commission has been long demanding 400 posts, including at its regional offices across the country. Despite this, the sanctioned posts have not been filled. Yet, most of these positions have been vacant over a period of time. The lack of manpower largely hampers the investigation process and the cases remain unresolved for long periods of time. Cases that are reported to the Commission have a conviction rate of less than 5 per cent.[51] Even the Twelfth Five Year Plan report on social sector mentions ways to strengthen the NCST through improvements in the functioning of the Commission and placement of requisite manpower at its headquarters and regional offices.

Because of this shortage of manpower, the Commission finds itself restricted as a monitoring body. It asks for reports and sends communication to state governments or any authority concerned, describing shortcomings noticed in implementation.

The lack of seriousness towards the Commission is reflected in the delay in the annual Action Taken Report (ATR) prepared by each state. State governments take a year or two to submit this report to the Commission. The report has to be presented in both the Houses of Parliament for discussion. So far, the commission has presented five reports to the president, while only three of them have been laid before Parliament.[52] Furthermore, state governments invariably fail to implement the Commission's recommendations as they are not mandatory.

The NCST also doesn't have a decisive role over the funds sanctioned under the TSP. Though it is an independent body, the funds are channelized through the Ministry of Tribal Affairs, affecting the autonomy of the commission. That's why the governments of Andhra Pradesh, Telangana and Karnataka framed an SCSP-TSP Act to curb the misuse or diversion of TSP. It would be expedient for other states to enact similar laws over which the NCST can play a key role.

A New Adivasi Policy: In 1999, the NDA government issued a draft National Policy on Tribals to address the developmental needs of tribal people.[53] Special emphasis was laid on education, forestry, healthcare, languages, resettlement and land rights. The draft policy sought to bring Scheduled Tribes into the mainstream of society through a multi-pronged approach for their all-round development without disturbing their distinct culture. A Cabinet Committee on Tribal Affairs (CCTA) was meant to constantly review the policy, but no steps have been taken in that direction. The CCTA rarely meets and the draft policy has not materialized into a functioning policy.

Even though the Constitution has provided for the socio-economic development and empowerment of Scheduled Tribes, there has been no defined national policy which could have helped translate the constitutional provisions into a reality. Therefore, the Ministry of Tribal Affairs must take adequate steps in the formulation of a National Policy on Scheduled Tribes.

The policy should be formulated by taking relevant stakeholders into confidence, such as tribal leaders, the state, organizations in the public and the private sectors and NGOs. The national policy must address the issues faced by tribals in a concrete way and enlist measures to be taken to preserve and promote tribal cultural heritage.

Countering the Hindutva Agenda

While reforming government policies, institutions and programmes are crucial, they will not automatically check the work of institutions such as ABVKA, who work towards subsuming Adivasi communities into the Hindu fold. That necessitates a political and ideological answer. Creating an organization that patiently and systematically works with Adivasis to understand (and fulfil) their needs and aspirations, to address their problems and socialize them to constitutional values is the only way forward. This would mean working away from the media glare and from the lure of electoral politics. Only when such an organization works on a mission mode can India hope to regain the hearts and minds of Adivasis.

Conclusion

Since India's Independence, the state's relationship with Adivasis has been strained to say the least. Having realized that they are getting marginalized in terms of their culture, social formation and economic rights, Adivasis have been raising demands for recognition to their rights and cultural identity. If Adivasis are to have any meaningful autonomy over their lands, a significant shift in the current legal framework is necessary. The only law that will return control and autonomy to tribes is one that envisions Adivasis not as encroachers, but as natural caretakers of the land. In the last few years, whatever progress had been made to further the promise of India to Adivasis has been undermined by the NDA. Earlier laws and policies designed to empower and uplift them have been systematically diluted or scrapped. The NDA has methodically undermined the rights of Adivasis, which in fact should be seen as inalienable rights. This points to the possibility of an increased interference in Adivasi forest habitats.

Dr Ambedkar had once argued that every citizen has claims on the fruits of prosperity and necessities of life. This means guaranteeing equal opportunities of growth to all Indians. Doing this means reinstating the rights-based paradigm and properly implementing the PESA, FRA and LARR Act. It means building on their successes, evolving new ways to extend autonomies and deepening the promise of India for Adivasis. Only then can India become a true beacon of hope and prosperity for peoples across the world.

Class Struggle and the Future of Adivasi Politics

Archana Prasad

Introduction

Jamlo, a 12-year-old Adivasi girl from Bastar, Chhattisgarh, died walking back to her home on 18 April 2020. When she died, she had already walked for most of the 200 km from the chilli fields of Telangana. She was only 55 km away from home. Jamlo's parents told the correspondent from the *People's Archives of Rural India* that they largely made their ends meet through paddy consumption and the sale of some forest produce.[1]

Most families in the central and eastern regions of the countries have similar stories because they are unable to eke out a living from their landholdings. This means Adivasis are 'farmers' for a few months and 'workers' for most part of the year. About two-thirds of Adivasi households can be classified as 'semi-proletarian' and the rest, barring a minuscule few, as the 'proletariat'.[2] This distinction needs to be made because, for the semi-proletariat the question of land is key, while the proletariat, it has often been argued, are more concerned with wages and social security in informal work. However, prominent scholars like Jan Breman[3] and Jens Lerche[4] locate Adivasis in the category of the 'labouring poor' for whom land does not seem to be a key issue. They contend that the era of the small peasantry is over and that we are living in a society where land has no importance for the most vulnerable labouring poor, as they largely depend on labour for their survival. This understanding, however, is only a partial representation of social reality, because possession and access to land remains a major focus for struggling Adivasis even today.

As is evident from Vikas Rawal's analysis of the National Sample Survey data (2013),[5] about 10 per cent of the Adivasis can be classed as 'landless peasants' or 'proletariat', who have no means of production. A majority (68.83 per cent) are in fact marginal peasants with land holdings between the size of 0.002 and 1.00 hectare. And about 15 per cent have been classed as small peasants occupying between one and two hectares of land. But it is well known that the produce from most of these lands does not even meet the basic needs of the Adivasi household. Hence, they are forced to work for others, either as migrants or as labour within the locality. It is estimated that in 2012–13, at least one person from about 79 per cent of marginal farmers and about 15 per cent of small Adivasi farmers went out of the village to search for work.[6] They can be identified as the 'semi-proletariat' within the larger economy.

The above-mentioned class position of more than 80 per cent of the Adivasis has arisen out of a peculiar contradiction that arose out of the Nehruvian approach to the Adivasis. In his 1953 speech, Jawaharlal Nehru argued for a humane and compassionate approach to the 'tribal people' and the slow introduction of 'developmental' measures which kept the culture and moral values of 'tribal life' intact. The five principles of administration, i.e., the tribal panchsheel, also highlighted the cultural specificity of Adivasi life and the need to 'preserve their culture' and respect their rights on forests and land, while slowly introducing and adapting modern values to Adivasi society.[7] These measures were in line with the legal framework that outlined protective measures, albeit without taking measures to restrict the penetration of oppressive economic forces into these regions. The contradiction within this vision lay in the fact that 'culture' and 'economy' were seen as two unrelated spheres of change. And though Nehru spoke of the need to avoid the museumization of 'tribal culture', his vision in fact led to the official perspective that indeed looked at 'Adivasi culture' as something that was unique and also their socio-economic condition as 'primitive', thus ignoring the inequities and injustices that defined the parameters of the 'Adivasi' question.[8]

The relationship of the Adivasis with the State and national capitalist development was further influenced by the paradigm of 'development' promoted by the ruling classes. By the time of Independence, the patterns of uneven development and conflict between classes in rural India had ensured that most Adivasi regions, especially of central and eastern India, were marginalized into living in thickly forested and mineral-rich districts. The government was the main owner of these resources and the special rights of the Adivasis over forests were defined through Schedules, until the enactment of the Forest Rights Act in 2006. The dispossession of Adivasis of their land because of the intensification of mining and big developmental projects is a phenomenon that has been present throughout the post-Independence period. However, the character of this dispossession changed substantially post the 1990s, largely because the protective Schedules and measures of affirmative action were repeatedly diluted by Union and state governments because of competing economic interests and political pressures.[9] There was also a substantial weakening of land acquisition laws and environmental laws, which were modified in favour of private parties.[10] Along with this, the deepening agrarian distress also exposed the underlying structural fault lines of the Nehruvian vision that guided policy makers for most part of the twentieth century.[11] Such developments have resulted in the formation of large labour reserves, where the most deprived sections of the workforce—Dalits and Adivasis being a majority in them—went out to towns, bigger villages and cities to look for work, especially with the increasing pace of the urbanization in the last two decades. The expansion of this mass of mobile men and women, which were largely contractual and casual labour, had implications for contemporary politics.

This essay considers the trajectories of Adivasi politics and its relations with working class movements in the light of the above-mentioned structural transformations. It argues that the long-term impact of systemic discrimination against the Adivasis can be captured in a discussion of two seemingly contradictory political trajectories. The first among these is the politics of Adivasi identity and the second, working class politics for Adivasi rights, both of which have a long historical lineage. All local and national level struggles may be located in different permutations and combinations within this broad spectrum. It delineates the complex interrelationships between these two macro-political tendencies and explores the possibilities of united action, which is essential to counter the growing power of capital. The essay explores the future prospects of a broader unity being forged between Adivasi and non-Adivasi workers, a goal that can only be attained if the Adivasis themselves are liberated from oppressive structures of contemporary capitalism.

Two Contrasting Images of Resistance

In recent times, two images have symbolized the diversity of the resistance strategies among the Adivasis: the first is the Pathalgadi movement for autonomy and the second, the Kisan Long March (2017–18) in Maharashtra of the All India Kisan Sabha which was dominated by the Adivasi peasantry. Both these movements symbolize the 'seemingly contradictory' tendencies that I have mentioned earlier. The Pathalgadi movement in Jharkhand is representative of one end of the spectrum, i.e., modern-day Adivasi identity politics. The Kisan Long March is an apt representation of class-based Adivasi politics. Here, I use both these movements as pegs to analyse the broader political implications of both these trends.

Coming first to Adivasi identity politics, movements such as the one in Pathalgadi have been demanding 'autonomy' and 'self-rule' since the 1980s under the Fifth Schedule and the Panchayat (Extension to Scheduled Areas) Act[12] of the Indian Constitution. This is their non-violent protest against the dilution of 'traditional' tenancy and land rights under successive governments. In the Pathalgadi movement, around seventy villages from Khunti district of Jharkhand barricaded their villages against intrusions of 'outsiders' with stones on which they inscribed their legal rights. The contemporary practice of barricading through stones has been projected as a 'traditional' practice for defending the village and its self-government. Accordingly, many villages announced their decision to recognize the sovereignty of Gram Panchayats and denounce the oppressive state laws which were diluting the Chotanagpur Tenancy Act (1908) that recognized rights of descendants on ancestral land in Jharkhand. But the use of a 'traditional' practice as a form of protest seemed to be only symbolic, because the most interesting part of the movement has been that villagers are expressing their allegiance to a modern-day Indian Constitution by inscribing their legal rights on stones. Therefore, their demand for sovereignty is not based on some historical antecedent, but highlights their own interpretation of the Constitution and the 'autonomy' granted under its provisions. The movement eventually spread to seventy villages and covered the three different states of Chhattisgarh, Madhya Pradesh and Odisha, apart from Jharkhand.[13]

This, however, is not an entirely new demand[14] and the struggles for 'autonomous control' have a long history, right from the movement for a separate Santhal state in the 1930s till the struggles for separate tribal states in the late twentieth century. In the North-east too, there were struggles for 'independence' and even greater autonomy[15], often resulting in ethnic clashes whose root cause seemed to be control over historical territories. Though vastly diverse in their regional and temporal spread, the strategies and character of such struggles have had some commonalities.[16] First, they have an exclusivist and culturally particularistic approach towards politics, which is guided by the norm of self-representation. This means only those who are born Adivasis can understand the feeling of alienation being felt by their communities. Second, such an idea culture also led to mythical historical reconstructions which linked Adivasis to particular occupations and space. Many struggles, like the one in Pathalgadi or the ethnic conflicts in different parts of the North-east, invoked a sense of place and history as a mobilization strategy. However, often, local solidarities became more important than communitarian identities. For example, the symbolism of the Niyam Raja in the landmark Niyamgiri struggle against Vedanta was representative of a number of Adivasi and non-Adivasi groups and not of any particular Adivasi group.[17] This showed that it was possible to create symbolism of the oppressed social classes without resorting to cultural exclusivism, but such a trajectory is almost always ignored by the ruling class-led Adivasi identity politics. The third characteristic is the idea of the moral superiority of the Adivasi society and a valorisation of community-based institutions. The discourse of an egalitarian and democratic society lies at the core of the mobilizing strategy against existing forms of domination. But this tendency has also led to a cultural revivalism for creating a larger political community, albeit whose potential to alter and overturn oppressive class relations is quite limited.[18] It is well known that many of these struggles were led by the erstwhile ruling classes among the tribal people and this was reflected in the nature of the symbolism itself. For example, the dominance of Mundari culture, Santhali vernacular vocabulary and several other social customs of larger tribes tends to obfuscate the voices of smaller tribal groups within such a political formation.[19] Further, the apparently egalitarian character of the Adivasis also ignores and obfuscates the trials, tribulations and burdens of Adivasi women. Any acknowledgement of this only shows that ruling class-led Adivasi identity politics is based on the creation of a hegemonic, imagined political community which was influenced by the social and ideological positioning of its leaders, many of whom got incorporated in the political and economic power structure at points in time. Further, unequal power relations within these social groups are pushed under the carpet by powerful socio-economic interest groups whose political location is often based on compromise and self-interest. Of course, as pointed out earlier, one cannot paint all Adivasi identity politics with the same brush; rather, an assessment of diverse movements should be based on the class position of the leadership and demands of each struggle. This is necessary to 'sift the chaff from the wheat' and identify the potentially transformative elements of Adivasi identity politics.

This brings us to the second tendency, where working class and peasantry-led struggles have seen the participation of a multitude of Adivasis. Many of these struggles are led by the Adivasis themselves and their long history has led to the formation of some of the oldest Adivasi organizations in the country.[20] The primary reason for this participation was located in the class position of the majority of the Adivasis, who had either been evicted from their lands or were marginal farmers who were forced to work for feudal authorities as slave labour. Their unity of purpose with other landless workers and semi-proletarianized peasants was evident with the Warli struggle led by Godavari Parulekar and the continuous organization of tribal people by the less-known movements of Tripura's Ganamukti Parishad and Kerala's Punnapra-Vayalar revolt.[21] It is important to note that these struggles were forced to engage with the question of identity and practice the politics that addressed the specific issues raised by the ideologues of Adivasi politics. While the agenda for land reforms and sharecropping rights attracted a large number of Adivasis, the need to counter social discrimination and address issues of land alienation, historical discrimination and right to self-government through respect for decentralized institutions was felt right through the 1970s and 1980s.[22]

But there was no one solution for these problems and different types of class-oriented movements tried different methods to resolve the issues arising out of the debate. For example, in Maharashtra's Thane district, Warli Adivasis were organized as dispossessed peasants, even though they occupied land through their historical land struggles. This was only possible because they did not possess a 'legal title' on the lands on which they had settled and were therefore united with other squatters and landless peasants. The specific needs of the Warlis were addressed through the formation of a social service organization, the Adivasi Mandal, which began to address the problems of health and education.[23] In other cases, worker's organizations leveraged the existing legal frameworks of affirmative action and protective legislation to organize Adivasis and Dalits. In Andhra Pradesh, student organizations organized students from Adivasi and Dalit social groups to address their specific concerns, even while linking it with the wider student movement. Similarly, the political movement for the Sixth Schedule in 'tribal majority' areas was led by the Ganamukti Parishad and the Communist Party of India (Marxist) in Tripura; however, such a struggle endeavoured to mobilize a wide spectrum of workers in order to achieve their goal. A different approach was followed by the Naxalites of the early 1970s who largely mobilized around class positions and worked amongst the Adivasi peasantry for the effective implementation of land reforms in West Bengal.[24]

The dynamics of class-based organizations entailed the democratization of the Adivasi consciousness, and these could be distinguished from other Adivasi struggles. Many struggles in Adivasi regions were embedded in movements for social transformation and which sought social, economic and political emancipation. This was evident in the programme of the All India Kisan Sabha which also worked among Adivasis in several areas without 'Adivasi' organizations. It was argued that the emancipation of the Adivasi peasantry lay at the heart of the resolution of the agrarian question and thus could not be separated from their social and political agenda.[25] Therefore, the formation of the local Kisan Sabha and Adivasi people's committees were preceded by the establishment of broad forums advocating social and cultural agendas. This meant that communitarian structures were replaced by people's committees with elected representatives. In this way they challenged the feudal and hegemonic influences of the ruling classes within the Adivasis, thereby attracting sharp criticism from several ideologues of Adivasi identity politics. This is seen in the oppositional politics of states like Kerala and Tripura, where the growth of the 'politics of indigeneity' tries to recreate the past in order to counter class-based mobilization.[26] Thus, historically speaking, though there appears to be a conflicting dynamic between class-based and identity-driven Adivasi politics, contemporary social reality projects a different picture. This is discussed in the next section.

Are These Differences Irreconcilable?

Contrary to popular opinion, the apparent contradiction between these two political trends is not irreconcilable and certainly cannot be generalized to arrive at a uniform simplistic conclusion. Rather, their destinies are intertwined with each other through the oppressive impact of the structural transformations that have taken place in the past few decades. The advent of neo-liberalism has created space for reactionary right-wing politics since the first decade of the twentieth century. Aggressive Hindutva (for example in the form of reconversion campaigns) in the post-Mandal period was accompanied by the ascendancy of neo-liberalism, which were vigorously pursued since the turn of the twentieth century by BJP governments at the Centre and in many states. Policies promoting the 'opening up' of Adivasi-dominated areas largely benefited the funders of RSS-affiliated organizations like Vanvasi Kalyan Ashram and Saraswati Shiksha Sansthan, a major part of whose funding came from local traders, big companies and foreign interests.[27] Thus, the activities of the Sangh Parivar and their ideologically affiliated governments have ended up strengthening rather than dismantling the very forces that have been exploiting the tribal people since the advent of British rule in these areas. This also resulted in communal polarization within Adivasi societies, where outfits associated with the Sangh have influenced changes in the character of Adivasi identity itself. For example, the Kandhamal riots of 2008 took a communal turn through the formation of a 'Hinduized tribal identity' under the influence of Hindutva forces. The conflict between Christian Dalits and the Kui and Kandh Hinduized tribals began with the Christian Pano demanding ST status. But the Kui samaj opposed this and received the full support of the Sangh leader, creating a communally polarized situation.[28] Other examples are the polarization and growing anti-Muslim sentiment among the Bodos in recent times. However, in many of these cases, the BJP and other Sangh affiliates have had to adapt their own politics to the dictates of the local community structure, reconfiguring both Hindutva as well as identity politics.[29]

Thus, we see that the reconfiguration of Adivasi identity politics is a necessary condition for expansion of the Hindutva project and this has altered the relationship between elites and workers within the Adivasi society. The old, hegemonic influence of communitarian elites seems to have waned to a considerable extent as many of them started cooperating with the mainstream Hindu nationalist agenda and also propagating neo-liberal policies as a panacea for solving the problems of ordinary Adivasis. Thus, often, Adivasi leaders from the ruling classes became collaborators in spreading the hegemonic influence of the BJP and even having political alliance with them, first in eastern India and currently also in the North-east, thus threatening the very existence of Adivasi identity politics.

Such communal polarization cannot be seen in isolation from the growing dispossession and economic crisis that is being faced by the Adivasis and which is reflected in a couple of important trends. First, the decision to open forest lands to acquisition by big private players; the rate of diversion of forests increased significantly between 2012 and 2018 by 10–15 per cent and resulted in the alienation of Adivasis from the land and in gaining access to forest resources.[30] This meant that most landless, marginal and small Adivasi peasants became dependent on agricultural and casual labour for their survival. The latest data shows that the rates of unemployment for the Dalits and Adivasis were among the highest in recent times, thus fuelling labour reserves in both urban and rural regions.[31] Second, the introduction of foreign investments in mining and infrastructural projects exacerbated the already existing direct conflicts between the local Adivasis and the corporates, with the State using force to repress these struggles for Adivasi rights. Third, the dilution of social welfare measures and protective legislations deepened the already existing institutional vacuum, thus leaving the door open for violent clashes and conflicts which, again, reflected a militaristic approach to the Adivasi question by the current ruling classes. One manifestation of this has been the direct confrontation between military forces and the 'Maoists' in central and eastern India, which resulted in the loss of life and livelihood of Adivasi inhabitants in forest highlands.

These developments have impacted both identity- and class-based Adivasi politics in significant ways, often leading to the changes in their content and socio-political character. As mentioned earlier, the ruling class politics of identity has received a clear setback, as Hindutva politics tried to incorporate it within its own fold. But this setback has resulted in a new type of Adivasi politics with a working-class leadership that has reached out to diverse social movements and organizations; many of these have been working class–oriented organizations and movements which have been forced to address the problems of social discrimination that have exacerbated under neo-liberalism. The most successful collaboration between 'Adivasi politics' and working-class/peasant organizations has been seen in the campaign to enact a socially just Scheduled Tribes and Other Traditional Forest Dwellers (Recognition of Forest Rights) Act, 2006 (or the Forest Rights Act, as it is popularly known). This Act widened the scope of rights to include people who were either displaced and or were living in national parks and sanctuaries. But above all, it attempted to democratize the rights settlement process by making panchayats responsible for the initiation of the process and laying down stringent conditions for the diversion of forest lands. Some of these radical and important provisions were mooted at the initiative of an alliance of organizations which opened up the process of legislation to public debate and forced negotiated changes. But the final version of the Act showed the power of the neo-liberal state which was able to insert some limiting provisions in the fine print to protect the interests of the forest bureaucracy, the conventional environmentalists and industry.[32]

Nevertheless, the entire process of forging a united campaign was instructive in showing what a common minimum consensus can achieve through an alliance of diverse forces. Consequently, there has been a consolidation of this ongoing alliance through a joint campaign for a socially just implementation of the Forest Rights Act. For example, when the Supreme Court, in a recent order dated 13 February 2020, ruled that all claimants whose rights have been rejected should be evicted from forest lands, a number of platforms for Adivasi rights came together to demand a review. In another instance, joint platforms built campaigns to oppose the dilution of the Scheduled Castes and Scheduled Tribes (Prevention against Atrocities) Act. The Union government was forced to give an assurance that the amendments would not be carried out. In part, these successes may also be seen as a result of changes in strategy by peasant and workers movements themselves.

For example, let us take the case of the Kisan Long Marches, the first of which was organized by the Maharashtra State Committee of the All India Kisan Sabha in March 2018. Inspired by its success, an All India Kisan Coordination Committee was formed, comprising more than 180 nationwide organizations. They initiated a Nationwide Kisan Long March in November 2019. What is significant is that all the regional and nationwide Kisan marches/agitations saw a large participation of Adivasi women, many of whom were marginal peasants and agricultural workers. Their participation was a result of persistent and deepening of agrarian distress, which resulted in mobility of more and more Adivasi workers who have been spending longer times of the year as migrants. A great number of these were Adivasi women who were not getting work within the agricultural sector. It is significant that in recent times (2012–18), the decline in the number of Adivasi women workers within urban areas is almost negligible compared to the sharp fall in employment in rural areas.[33] This has brought about a greater convergence of interests between the Adivasis and other workers who, apart from the landless, also comprise middle, small and marginal landholders. In other words, the large-scale, semi-proletarianization of all segments of the peasantry created some unity of purpose between Adivasis and the larger peasantry. Thus, the deepening economic crisis—which has manifested itself in the burgeoning employment crisis—has provided some unity of purpose to different segments of the working classes. An illustration of this has been seen in the very large participation of the Adivasi peasants in several peasant protests, including the Kisan Long March.

Class-based organizations have also intensified their work among the Adivasi people; several demands for regularization of rights in forested regions and social protection for Adivasis have entered class organizations, many of whom have also begun to develop leadership in sectors with a preponderance of Adivasi workers. But these adjustments in strategies involved a difficult set of negotiations, where class perspectives had to reconcile with the persistence of Adivasi identity politics, which in part is structured by the policies of the State itself, which in the last few decades, has increasingly facilitated the introduction of corporate capital in nature-rich Adivasi regions.[34]

These changing constellations of protest have, however, got their own fault lines; the most prominent of them being on the question of the strategies and tactics of the 'Maoists', the space for whose violent politics has been created by the structural violence of the State itself. The greater absence of the State in developmental works after the 1990s has been accompanied by the persistent opening up of Bastar to corporate players through the development of limited infrastructure. The resultant conflict led to the military fortification of the region on which a multitude of Adivasi and tribal organizations have had diverse positions. Among many diverse positions, one perspective treats the 'Maoists' as the voice of the Adivasis and another treats the Adivasis as victims of both Maoist and State violence. A third position adopts a human and democratic rights approach, seeing the emergence of violent politics as a symbol of a systemic crisis which got accentuated in the current phase of capitalism. Except for the first, neither of these are mutually exclusive and many of these positions overlap with each other in order to respond to conflict situations.[35] This is seen in joint campaigns on state atrocities and targeting of Adivasis as 'Maoists' in recent times, once again showing that there are new possibilities for cooperation between different Adivasi and workers organizations in contemporary India.

Concluding Remarks

This essay has provided a broad overview of the trajectories of contemporary Adivasi politics and highlighted a necessity for taking up issues on a joint platform. In the past, conventional political discourse has seen class-based and Adivasi identity politics as antithetical to each other. However, the social and political reality is far more complex than the one presented by this polarized discourse and the systemic tendencies of semi-proletarianization have structured this duality in politics. But as argued here, the multifarious manifestations of neo-liberal policies have also created diverse forms of Adivasi politics with different social basis. It is therefore important to distinguish between identity-based struggles which have been led by those who are situated within the working class and those whose motive has been to get incorporated within the current power structure. Further, the culturally exclusive character of Adivasi politics is also hegemonic and camouflages the inequalities within Adivasi society. On the other hand, non-culturally exclusive class politics has had to come to terms with the persistence of identity-based politics by adopting a more nuanced approach towards it. This collaboration has been facilitated by the intensifying communal polarization and economic crisis, leading to the transformation of Adivasi politics, both class and identity based. Such a development is not only positive, but also essential to take on an authoritarian and neo-liberal government and the challenges that it poses to all progressive forces within the country.

Lessons from the Institution of 'Indigenous Self-Governance'

Vincent Ekka

Abstract

The 'Parha' system is a traditional way of self-governance among the Kurux (Oraon) Adivasis of central India. Similar institutions of traditional self-governance are in operation among other major tribal communities of central India and across the globe. Highlighting the aspects of 'effective local self-governance' in traditional institutions such as the Parha, this essay will strive to underline various regressive forces that hinder the growth and practice of tribal self-governance in a free and fair manner. This essay will also attempt to communicate with non-indigenous society, the lessons that can be learnt from these traditional 'tribal/indigenous institutions of self-governance' and why autonomy through tribal self-governance could be a better option for our forests and rivers.

Introduction

In the present economic and political structures, the use of natural resources is made essential. Natural resources like water, land, forest, etc., have always been essential for human survival, but they have never been exploited on such a massive scale before. Natural surroundings have also helped shape human cultures down the centuries. These socio-cultural resources of a community are as essential to human existence as natural resources. They are important for the progress, development and sustainability of any community. The much-acclaimed socio-cultural resources of indigenous communities are ecological sensitivity, community-centeredness, harmonious co-existence with nature, economy in land use, life-giving aspects of feasts and celebrations and institutions of self-governance such as Parha, Doklo, Manki Pir, Pargana, etc. Other value-based socio-cultural resources are bisu sendra (annual ceremonious hunting), parha jatra (annual social gathering of Parha villages), jani shikar (women's ritual hunting), etc. Indigenous communities and cultures in other parts of globe have similar socio-cultural resources such as ubuntu (in African indigenous communities); sumak kawsay, buen vivir, suma qamana, etc., (in South American indigenous communities) and the concept of Gross National Happiness in Bhutan. The present article will extensively deal with the socio-cultural institution of Parha in the central Indian tribal region and how relevant lessons can be drawn from the traditional self-governance system for authentic human living.

What is the Parha System?

Parha is a cluster of villages in a particular area. The number of villages in Parhas may differ; for example, there are Parhas consisting of seven, eight, ten, twelve or twenty-one villages known as 7 Parha, 8 Parha, 10 Parha, 12 Parha and 21 Parha, respectively. Parha is a socio-cultural-political institution of self-governance for the well-being of the Adivasi community living in the region. Each Parha works in an autonomous fashion, though they follow the same kinds of customary rights. There are office bearers in each Parha named differently in different Adivasi communities of the central Indian regions.

Name of the Tribe	System	Head of the Parha
Oraon	Parha–patti	Parha Belas
Munda	Parha	Munda Raja
Santhal	Pargana	Parganait
Ho	(Manki) Pir[1]	Manki Pir
Kharia	Doklo	Doklo Sohor

There are other office bearers in each Parha, such as the Parha Dewan, Parha Kotwar and Parha Salahkar. Here the office bearers are not just individuals; the entire village is designated as Raja gaon, Dewan gaon, Kotwar gaon, Salahkar gaon, etc. Though the office bearers are individuals, their whole village is assigned the responsibilities. Similarly, not only the office-bearing villages, but all the villages within a Parha are given particular names, as the following image (Figure 1) illustrates 12 Parha:

Figure 1: The 12 Parha

Each Parha has a Parha chief who is called Parha Raja or Munda Raja or Parganait or Manki Pir or Doklo Sohor. The Parha system functions in tribes with some differences. This system of local self-governance is inclusive of people of other cultures and communities as well.

Unlike the Oraon tribe's Parha system that functions within a cluster of villages, the Munda tribe has clusters formed according to clans. Thus, they have Parhas like 12 mauja Sanga Parha, 24 mauja Guria Parha, 22 mauja Topno Parha and so on. Here, Sanga, Guria and Topno are the names of different clans. This is possible because different villages are settled according to different clans.

The Role and Function of the Parha Raja

The role and function of the Parha Raja and other officials, as well as each village, is defined for the smooth functioning of a Parha. The role and function defined to a Parha village is a designation given to the village; the consideration of hierarchy is not at work but it is just a division of labour to be carried out. In a field interview, Simon Oraon, the Parha Raja of 12 Parha said, 'Nobody is high or low in a Parha. All are equal. But for proper functioning of the Parha, the Parha Raja, Dewan, Kotwar and Salahkar are selected from the villages.' Though individuals are selected for the office of the Parha, the whole village is responsible for particular, assigned jobs. The Parha Raja never works as an individual but as a representative of an institution.

The chief functions of the Parha Raja are:

- To solve all kinds of disputes within the Parha.
- To deliver justice.
- To maintain peace and harmony in the Parha.
- To maintain and promote social and cultural institutions.
- To lead the annual social functions of Bisu Sikar and Parha Jatra and other cultural practices.

Similarly, the functions of all other Parha officials are broadly defined. The function of the Parha Dewan is to exercise the role of a General Secretary in modern understanding and keep record of all that happens within the Parha. The Parha Dewan is considered the right-hand person of the Parha Raja in all matters. The role of a Kotwar is to pass on information. If any important and urgent message is to be communicated, the whole Kotwar village carries out the duty. The fourth official in a Parha is Salahkar, whose duty is to provide sound advice to the Parha Raja and other officials. For the above-mentioned offices, the people in the village select a trustworthy person upon whom they can place their confidence. There is no fixed time for the change of Parha officials. It depends on how long the people want their Parha officials to continue in office. On the other hand, Parha officials are free to resign any time from their office and the office remains functional until the resignation is accepted by the people.

A similar practice is at work in the Kolhan region[2] among the Hos and other tribals. According to the Ho and Santhal tribe, the cluster-wise system of self-governance is called Pir and Pargana and the people in authority are called Manki Pir and Parganait respectively. Among the Ho tribe, the village head is called Munda[3] and a person in authority at a cluster level (Pir) is called Manki or Manki Pir. The rights and duties of the Munda and Manki, besides the above-mentioned functions like that of the Kurux (Oraon) Parha Chief, include the right to 'settle wastes',[4] collect revenue, arrange for and maintain natural irrigation sources and fallows, act as police head for his village/Pir and maintain law and order, engage in social forestry and protect protected forests and reserved forests (Sundar: 2005). The Kolhan region seems to be in a better position in terms of defining and empowering its traditional village headmen than the Munda or Oraon tribes of other areas. Wilkinson's Rule[5] (1837), still in force for the Kolhan, provided for disputes to be settled by local Panchayats and prohibited lawyers. In the rest of Chotanagpur too, the rights and obligations of village headmen are part of the record of rights of each village under Chapter XV, Section 127 of the Chotanagpur Tenancy (CNT) Act, 1908. Their duties are similar to that of Ho Mundas[6]. However, unlike the recognition given by Indian laws to Ho Mankis and Santhal Parganaits, there is no formal recognition of the offices in the Parha system of the Mundas and Oraons. Moreover, there was no provision of remuneration for the Munda and Oraon village heads, while a symbolic remuneration of Rs 75–100 was given to the Mankis and Mundas of 26 Pir in the Kolhan region until 1992 (Sundar 2005).

In most cases, the indigenous Parha system of local governance is compatible with the Constitution of the nation under 'the customary law'. The customary laws and the Parha system have legal and constitutional sanction to ensure the well-being or good living of the Adivasis and other communities residing in Scheduled areas. Parha culture has the potential to initiate alternative human practices which, in sophisticated terms, can be named as development practices. However, the philosophical nature of the indigenous Parha culture needs to be explored further for greater compatibility, transparency and sustainability. The positive side of the system is that it gives an active view of citizenship, where the residents of a Parha strongly feel a sense of belonging to it and thereby enjoy the citizenship rights and privileges within it. This imbues people with notions of self-governance, accountability and responsibility. The Parha as an Adivasi system of self-governance has the capacity for organizing, managing and directing the community. It ensures the protection and promotion of community-owned resources.

Another striking feature of the Parha is that though the administrative work is time- and energy-consuming, all the offices are unpaid offices, including that of the Parha Raja. In today's world, it is really noble to exercise the offices and duties of a Parha gratis. It can be said that the Parha system is one of the highest forms of democratic principles in practice. The three vital pillars of a democracy—legislature, judiciary and executive—are found in this Adivasi system of village administration.

It is said that customary rights arise from specific socio-economic circumstances. Customary governance structures like the Parha system or Pargana system are based on local identities: ethnic, religious or clan based. The customary governance structures and practices are developed for the smooth functioning and welfare of the community. Like the Parha (Oraon and Munda), Pargana (Santhal), Manki Pir (Ho) and Doklo (Kharia), many other Adivasi communities of India and indigenous communities across the globe have developed customary governance structures and practices that they call by different names. In Latin America, for example, the suma qamana in the Bolivian Aymara language and sumak kawsay (buen vivir) in the Ecuadorian Quichua language; in Bhutan, the indigenous governance structure is known as Gross National Happiness and ubuntu (Zulu language) in African customary practices. All these concepts create alternative possibilities of a good life. They are systems of indigenous self-governance for the well-being of indigenous communities living in the region. The systems include peoples of other cultures as well. The indigenous Parha culture is the actual site of cosmo-political cultures when it enters into contact with wider cultural avenues. The indigenous Parha culture, with its autonomous practices of self-governance, possesses the potency for judicial, legislative and executive capabilities. The fundamental values enshrined in the indigenous Parha cultures have universal applicability. There is a mutual support system based on the communitarian well-being of all that is open to universal needs and co-operation.

However, in spite of many good aspects, the Parha system is not foolproof, which means the modern understanding of human rights, gender justice and gender equality apparently do not appear in the system and practice. The customary self-governance structures may often be fragmented and incoherent in terms of modern political structures, but they have basic systems of justice delivery and reconciliation mechanisms. In this regard Kennedy (2016) makes an observation, 'In so far as it constitutes an internal process of dialogue, action, reflection and change, the indigenous model has come to be characterized by a strong tendency to make use of the local community's own resources, and therefore commands a considerable degree of credibility, participation and sustainability.' Not much study and research has gone into the customary practices and indigenous self-governance structures and their functions. There is a dearth of organized academic pursuit. Hence, the integration between the customary and formal structure is far from reality. Moreover, there is no mechanism developed to incorporate the customary structures into prevailing governance structures. An ambitious attempt was made in India through the provisions of the PESA 1996, which was meant to take into account local self-governance systems while ensuring decentralization of power and governance. But the political will to transfer power while talking about decentralization of power and governance is missing. This is the basic flaw of top-down approach as observed by Kennedy and his collaborators (2016): 'In this exogenous approach, the decisions made from outside the community have been found to be largely ineffective in changing established attitudes, beliefs and practices. The target community feels as if the externally driven development initiative is being imposed upon them. Thus as a development strategy, the 'top-down' model tends to underestimate the target community's ability to shape their own destiny.'

The traditional institutions that enjoyed a formal status in the pre-colonial era have been left to die a natural death in the modern political and economic structures of governance. The colonial West imposed their ideology and culture that 'represented the veritable emergence of a "new world", one that challenged the existing sense of time, space, laws, knowledge and social organization and that opened a new path of power, knowledge and being not only for Europe but gradually for the largest part of humanity' (Nelson 2012). The colonial modifications during the British Raj and state intervention in the post-Independence era have weakened and devalued the power of traditional self-governance structures.

If the resources for good governance are tapped from the indigenous Parha cultures, they can present alternative democratic governance in keeping with the United Nations' visions based on human rights, social justice and ecological sensitivities. Traditional structures need to be restored as 'units of social, political and economic self-governance'. In their book aptly titled *Building Communities from the Inside Out*, Kretzmann and McKnight (1993) argue that the process of recognizing the people's capacity to solve their own problems begins with the construction of a new lens through which communities can begin 'to assemble their strengths into new combinations, new structures of opportunity, new resources of income and control, and new possibilities for production'.

Conclusion

The Parha culture of indigenous self-governance invites humanity to a 'new citizenship' which would have to rethink and strive for a society based on gender justice, equality, ecological sensitivity and lack of discrimination, where all citizens of a Parha would conduct themselves in the true sense of social, economic and political fair-dealing. A healthy environment creates a healthy community free from sickness, famine, depravity and calamity which is a sign of harmonious co-existence. A healthy community and environment would mean a human and ecological community free from corruption, injustice and exploitation. The traditional Parha system of self-governance can provide such a perspective of co-existence. The most practical ideas and strategies with respect to interrelations, mutual dependence and co-existence can be learnt from indigenous worldviews. It has the potency of offering an alternative system of governance that aims at the general well-being of all. The system believes that well-being does not come by material growth alone. The Parha system provides a system compatible to modern democratic systems of governance and self-management of community and resources. Land is not a commodity or a thing but is connected with the existence and continuation of living beings. The spiritual vision of indigenous life can show a way for harmonious co-existence. The Parha system of self-governance tells that all life forms are equal and inter-connected; hence, they should be respected and not exploited. Community participation in ecological conservation can do wonders when there is a shared ownership of natural resources. The entire philosophy of life of the Parha system of self-governance believes that 'being more is better than having more'.

Silent Voices, Distant Dreams: India's Denotified Tribes

Ajay Dandekar

In the nineteenth century, the colonial government came to the dubious decision that nomads, itinerant traders and other wandering groups, along with those who were part of the disbanded armies of the principalities and kingdoms now under residencies, were structurally different from the settled agriculturists. These varying groups, communities and people could not be located within preconceived administrative, economic and social categories. They were therefore designated as factors within a predictable and tractable human landscape which had to be 'controlled' through legal and penal institutions for the maintenance of 'law and order'. This became the explanation for the enactment of the Criminal Tribes Act (CTA) of 1871. About 200 communities were notified by the British government as 'Criminal Tribes' by using the 1871 Act and its subsequent transformations. We need to retrace a bit in time to understand why the colonial government came to such a dubious conclusion which, at one stroke, defined people born in certain communities as 'criminals' and thus had to be treated differently. In order for us to retrace the path, we need to really understand two gentlemen of the yesteryears who, between themselves, created the great myth of the thuggee.

The first section of this essay will look at the possible antecedents and circumstances that led to the creation of the CTA. In subsequent sections, we will analyse the evolution of the Act followed by the post-Act context after 1948.

I

The notion of criminality and the so-called Criminal Tribes Act were formulated based on past experiences of a particular kind of crime that was associated with a particular slang term from the colonial period, the thuggee. The initial investigation about this strange phenomenon was done by Thomas Perry,[1] though he did not reach the same conclusions as were later reached. For that we had to wait for the arrival of two gentlemen, Captain Philip Meadows Taylor and Captain William Sleeman.[2]

Along with Captain Sleeman, it was the explorer, administrator and fiction writer Captain Philip Meadows Taylor to whom we should turn to understand the phenomenon of the thuggee. Taylor did not belong to the upper crust of English society of gentlemen in the strictest sense of the term. He was not to the manor born as it were and was not a product of Oxford and Cambridge. He was not a member of that upper class of Englishmen who, as if by right, occupied the high positions of power. As a young man he landed in Bombay in 1924, eager to prove himself and earn a livelihood as well as fame. Captain Taylor himself recalled a conversation with an astrologer who said he would never be rich, but fame would certainly be his. He wrote fiction depicting contemporary Indian rulers, described archeological findings explored by the colonial archeologists of his time and presented India through his writing as an explorer would a foreign land. Taylor spent a significant amount of time in Shorapur, a small principality of the Berads, as a resident. From his rather cozy mansion that overlooked the rock-strewn

Shorapur—home to the tough Berads who had fought the Mughal Emperor Aurangzeb to a standstill—Taylor conceptualized many of his projects. One of them took the form of a novel which he himself claimed was truth fictionalized. Thus, was born *Confessions of a Thug,* a dark story where the protagonist Ameer Ali gave an account of his life of impersonal killing as a professional Thug. The novel became so famous that even the queen of England could not wait for the pages to come out of the press and read them. Thus, Taylor laid claim for the discovery of the phenomenon.

However, it was another Captain (finally retired as a Colonel, Sleeman still lives in the memory of central India where a town is named after him) who gave the thuggee a legal face, did voluminous documentation and pursued the agenda of elimination of thuggees as a mission of his life. He was to claim that he had freed the land of the 'menace'.[3] But did the phenomenon exist?

Hiralal Gupta (1959, pp. 169–177) attributes the development of banditry in the early nineteenth century to the East India Company's expansionist policy. He suggests that a significant number of people captured as 'thugs' by the Department of Thuggee and Dacoity in the 1830s and 1840s were perhaps wandering soldiers of rulers whose states were now being controlled by the British. The wandering mercenary soldiers would have become a threat to the stability that the company rule sought and thus, something had to be done about it.

As David Arnold points out, 'To the colonial regime crime and politics were almost inseparable: serious crime was an implicit defiance of state authority and a possible prelude to rebellion; political resistance was either a "crime" or the likely occasion for it.'[4]

It has been argued that the large number of marauding groups in competition for political power and patronage in the late eighteenth century were seen as potential threats to the revenue generation and the very stability of the system. Such a threat must have necessitated the need to find an alternative source of revenue. Those characterized as 'thugs' were 'locally recruited, locally based' groups hired to carry out raids outside the immediate vicinity of a territory in order to make up for revenue that might have been lost to larger marauding groups.[5] These were controlled by the local rulers competing for revenue and thus extending patronage to the marauding groups that led to the phenomenon in the first place.

The most trenchant critique of the thuggee phenomenon comes from Parama Roy. She cogently argues that it was essentially a construct, the production of a colonial enterprise. Roy carefully dissects the construct of thuggee and shows it for what it was, a creation of the colonial project in the pursuit of governing the expanding empire in which the enterprise also needed to define the other clearly.[6]

'Thugs' thus were not a stereotype, but 'were gradually envisioned as a rebel force that threatened the stability of British rule. In a direct linkage to the Criminal Tribes legislation, rebellion or its potential structured the conceptual category of the other who was outside the law' (Mike Dash 2006, p. 29). Organized challenges to the Company's authority constituted a threat to it in this period as it began to assert its paramountcy following the final defeat of the Marathas in 1819. It is interesting to note in this context that the Indian Penal Code (IPC) and Criminal Procedure Code (CrPC) were adopted by the Raj in 1860 even before Britain itself had one. The 'Jewel in the Crown' was a laboratory for legislative and governance experiments.[7]

In fact, we may suggest that the CTA, implemented for colonial power, logically followed from the earlier construction of the thuggee and thus the notorious Thuggee Act became the precursor to the one that followed it, the CTA of 1871.[8] This endeavour to label communities in categories was largely a part of the discourse of the then anthropology of the west. Indeed, anthropology, primarily an academic discipline, became an instrument of colonial domination. It presented an oversimplified depiction of the cultural 'others' and, based on it, developed a perspective that made them appear as 'the opposite' of civilized British folks. Therefore, in those anthropological studies, the interpretation and description of Indian communities became a component in the political discourse of the day.[9] Eventually, to use a phrase of Antonin Gramsci, it became possible for an opposite view to emerge, underscoring 'contradictory consciousness'.[10]

It was thus a logical step in the construction of reality in the colonial mindset to create the infamous Act of 1871 that would now combat the raging notions of criminality constructed by the colonial state itself. This was followed by a series of Acts in 1897, 1911 and 1924. For all intents and purposes, the Criminal Tribes Act 1924 became the final act as it consolidated the entire legislation spread across various areas of the empire into one single act leading towards a law.

II

The CTA of 1871[11] was the beginning of a series of legislative injunctions which followed a similar pattern. Legal interventions of a similar type followed this Act at regular intervals so as to fine-tune it, elaborate upon it and extend its jurisdiction to make increasingly 'finer' distinctions between those people considered 'criminal' and those regarded as 'non-criminal'. The classification of communities considered 'criminal' was fairly broad-based, with the Act describing them in such terms as 'a tribe, gang or class'. The colonial masters did not wish to take any risks and leave any loopholes in their mode of categorization. None of these traveling communities could be situated within any of the preconceived categorizations according to which the colonial administration had previously classified different communities. In 1874, for example, there was a further amendment to the Act which sought to fine-tune this 'criminalized' category even further as follows: 'In this Act the words "tribe", "gang" and "class" shall be deemed to include any portion or members of a tribe, gang or class'. A range of social groups, who had lost their traditional occupations due to changes in the political and economic contexts in the colonial period and had resorted to taking up the issue with the erstwhile colonial masters, were all categorized as 'criminal tribes'. This categorization concealed the whole range of their social history antecedent to this colonial experience of the subcontinent and projected them as a singular mystic and homogenized category. The grouping of castes, tribes and communities for the purpose of formulating the CTA of 1871 came a little before the subsequent listing of 'Tribes' and 'Castes' by various colonial ethnographers.

The CTA, earlier applicable in the Central Province and the North-West Province, now included Bengal in its spread. Around the same time, both the Bombay and Madras Presidencies adopted the CTA for their own use in controlling 'criminal tribes'. The Bombay Presidency, like the United Provinces, had also been acquainted with the notion that the 'hereditary' criminals belonging to 'tribes' were a threat to law and order as early as 1827. There was a Regulatory Order passed to control them.

The colonial government's antipathy towards these communities was shared by the elite classes within the settled indigenous communities, as they were part of the hierarchical social network and political economy, while these wandering communities were not seen to belong to any known framework of social reference. This suspicious attitude towards unknown 'jatis' who periodically shared their territorial spaces froze into rigid statements of dislike when—added to their indeterminate caste characteristics—the CTA of 1871 added the stigma of criminality to these wandering communities. It was only after Independence that the unconstitutional nature of the designation 'criminal tribes' was recognized and the communities that had come under the purview of the Act were 'Denotified'.

The major provisions of the CTA, as noted above, provided for the registration of all declared criminal tribes. All members of criminal tribes had to report to the authorities at regular intervals and had to inform the authorities if they were to absent themselves from their residences for a day or more! For journeys outside settlements, special passes were required and any tribal member caught without a pass outside the settlement was to be imprisoned. All members of a declared criminal tribe had to answer a special roll call, which could take place at any random and unscheduled hour. If any member failed to respond, the onus was on the missing person to prove to the officer-in-charge at the settlement that his/her absence from residence involved no criminal acts or intentions.

Under the various acts passed and finally—through a consolidation of all the legislations in the Act of 1924—the colonial government also paved the way for opening up various settlements of the so-called criminal tribes. These were barbed wire-fenced camps where, according to the degree of 'criminality' perceived, the communities and persons were confined. Bombay Presidency alone had more than forty-four settlements, the biggest of them in the textile town of Sholapur. In fact, most of the settlements, at least in Bombay Presidency, were located in areas around either a textile centre, an industrial one or around large construction work areas.

Below, we produce a typical picture of a typical settlement, as described by the Settlement Commissioner of Bombay Presidency, Colonel Starte:[12]

'The total population in the settlements in the Bombay Presidency is 12,861. This shows an increase of 799. The list of the larger settlements with a population of over 1000 is as under:

Sholapur	4095
Indi	204
Bijapur	1229
Special Settlement	143
Bagalkot	397
Gadag	1023
Hubli	2322

Dharwar	405
Khanapur	548
Gokak Falls	672
Dandeli	251
Baramati	521

Primary education is compulsory for all the boys and girls between the ages of 5 and 12 years, and for all the children who work as half timers, in mills as long as they are half timers. In the latter case, therefore their half time attendance in the day school is compulsory until they reach the age of fifteen years. The following table is illuminating from the point of view of education:

Sholapur	4095	890
Indi	204	30
Bijapur	1229	230
Special Settlement	143	32
Bagalkot	397	66
Gadag	1023	194
Hubli	2322	457
Dharwar	405	39
Khanapur	548	65
Gokak Falls	672	182
Dandeli	251	29
Baramati	521	65
Nira Projects	630	112

In the sphere of vocational training, the various trades for which the training was imparted are as under: Carpentry (78), Masonry (92), Tailoring (7), Agriculture (22), Black Smith (3) and Weaving (4). The credit societies established in the settlements have continued their steady expansion and are in a good financial position. They serve a very useful purpose in providing loans for marriages and other expenses for the settlers. Some of them also finance and control carpentry factories attached to the settlements, and undertake building construction also. The share capital is now 10,405 compared with the 8846 for the last year, and total of deposits is 48,069 and the reserve funds are 9475.

Convictions and Absconders

The number of convictions is about the same as last year. The number of absconders remaining untraced on March 31st 1924 is 142, which is also about the same as the last year. This figure includes women and children, as settlement work deals with families, as whole and hence absconding dependents have to be brought back as well as the heads of the families. It is however only the men (69) and a few of the 44 women who are likely to engage in crime whilst they are absconding. The total number in the settlements is now 12,861. They are not confined to the settlements in the daytime. Hence, only about one percent is absconding.'

There was, thus, a tinge of welfare measures attached to the settlements and a sentiment of 'reform'. These settlements are still remembered with fond nostalgia. This is a telling indictment of the failure of independent India to make the lives of Denotified tribes any more secure or dignified. In a collaborative study conducted by me[13], we were fortunate enough to interact with one of the original residents of the settlement who was born in the settlement. He took us around the Sholapur settlement area. 'The British rule was far better! We had schools, we had a job and we were getting a dignified living. We were at peace in the settlement,' the gentleman said, as he nonchalantly waved at the vast brooding expanse of the barren landscape where the barbed wire fencing once stood. He could vividly recount the houses, the observatory and above all the towering figure of Starte Sahib who used to visit them on a horse with a posse of retainers. The conversation with him revealed certain interesting insights. He showed us an official document dated a couple of years ago, in which, opposite his name, the official concerned had written 'Criminal tribe' by hand. It seemed to him that independent India had betrayed them.

III

The 'tryst with destiny' for these communities did not come with Independence. While the rest of the country celebrated and bled on 15 August, the Notified Tribes languished in the settlements, still governed by the CTA of 1924 as well as the Habitual Offenders Act in some presidencies of the erstwhile Raj. Soon after Independence, in 1949, a committee was appointed under the chairmanship of Shri Ananthasayanam Ayyangar to, 'inquire in the workings of the Criminal Tribes Act of 1924 in the provinces; and to make recommendations for its modifications or repeal'.

Some of the observations of the committee make a fascinating reading. It sketched the historical background as evocatively as possible.

'In the first half of the 19th century, Northern India was overrun by thugs and dacoits. The population in general was much distributed and did not feel secure. The Government of India had therefore to take special measure to meet the situation and systematic operations to suppress the terrible crimes committed by the thugs were started in 1830. In 1839, the work of suppressing dacoity was also entrusted to a newly created Thug and Dacoity Department, which succeeded in suppressing the heinous crimes to a great extent.[14] The committee unanimously recommended to the Government of India that the CTA of 1924 be repealed. This historic recommendation however had also the proviso that 'Criminal Tribes Act should be replaced by a Central legislation applicable to all habitual offenders without any distinction based on caste, creed or birth and newly formed States included in Parts B and C of the First Schedule to the Constitution, which have local laws for the surveillance of the Criminal Tribes, should be advised to replace their laws in this respect by the Central legislation for habitual offenders, when passed'.[15] Thus, at the dawn of Independence— when the Criminal Tribes Act was being abolished—a backdoor entry was being granted to it by the compulsory enactment of the Habitual Offenders' Act.

Despite repeated campaigns and struggles that the Denotified tribes have put up since then, the state shows no intention of doing away with the spirit of the Act, whose ghost hovers above the communities in the name of the Habitual Offenders' Act. It can be seen that the colonial government's antipathy towards these communities was shared by those 'settled' Indian communities, who were part of the 'mainstream' and hierarchical social networks and political economy, as opposed to these wandering communities of 'tribals' who were not seen as belonging to any acknowledged framework of social reference. Of course, these tribal communities had been either forest-based communities or nomadic artisans and traders before they were categorized (or notified) as 'criminal' tribes during the colonial period. Today, many of these communities have lost their traditional, niche occupations as a consequence of social change and increased urbanization and economic industrialization. The Banjaras, for instance, have lost their traditional role as long-distance traders due to the huge changes which have taken place in relation to transport technology and enhanced road networks.[16] In a similar manner, those artisan communities who traditionally survived as craftsmen and artisans of various types are fast losing their importance within the rural economies of today. Pardhis in western and central India have lost their forest ecology due to deforestation and strict new policies as applied to the cultivation of forested areas. These communities are left with few other choices than assimilation with new forms of economy by taking on 'new' work practices.

There have been attempts to retrieve some ground with various communities and their leaderships coming together on some stated agenda. These attempts have yielded positive results in a number of ways. There has been greater self-awareness within the communities about their own rights and entitlements as well the government of the day also taking cognizance of the issues of stigma, of absence of constitutional protection and atrocities that the communities face. As a result, there have been a number of commissions appointed by the Government of India (GoI) to delve into the issue of the stigma as well as constitutional protection for communities who were declared by the colonial rule as criminal tribes. Notable among recent initiatives have been two reports, one by the Technical Advisory Group (TAG) appointed by the Government of India which submitted its report in 2006 and the other is the National Commission for Denotified, Nomadic and Semi-Nomadic Tribes (NCDNT) report submitted in 2008. The Ministry of Social Justice and Empowerment constituted the NCDNT in November 2003 which was reconstituted in March 2005. The major recommendations of both the reports pertained to:

1. Amendment to the Constitution.
2. Reservation in government jobs.
3. Action to be taken by states.
4. Action to be taken by GoI.
5. Action to be taken by both GoI and states.

The most recent policy discussion on the issue of the Denotified tribes and the reports mentioned above happened in the arena of the National Advisory Council (NAC) and is worth taking note of.

The NAC Working Group draft report analysed the TAG as well as the Commission report and also held its own consultation as well as a national consultation over one year. It recognized that there are several DNT communities in existence in India that deserved to be either in the list of STs or in the list of SCs, yet were not included in either list. It stated, 'The Denotified and Nomadic Tribes (DNTs) face special problems of their own and therefore need to be given focused attention by the Central Ministries and the State Governments. Among the Denotified Tribes, 58 per cent have been classified as SC/ST whereas 39 per cent are categorized as OBCs. Likewise, among the nomadic communities, 55 per cent are classified as SC/ST and 29 per cent are classified as OBCs. In all, 16 per cent of Nomadic communities and 3 per cent of Denotified Tribes are not classified as SC/ST or OBCs, as such, they do not get any benefits whatsoever. Even the ones who are covered are generally not able to avail of the benefits as SCs/STs/ OBCs because of either not having caste certificates, or because the quotas are cornered by the non-DNT communities in the reserved categories. Moreover, there are a number of States which have not made lists of either the Denotified or Nomadic communities and the status of such people is unknown and hence they constitute a deprived lot. Furthermore, due to their social background as erstwhile "Criminal Tribes", the DNTs face social stigma and are denied of many benefits which are given to SCs/STs and OBCs.' While the NAC working group accepted some key issues such as the abolition of the Habitual Offenders Act and extension of the ambit of the Atrocity Act, it however, shied away from supporting both the TAG as well as the Commission's fundamental recommendation of inclusion of the communities which the British had declared as criminal tribes into either a separate Schedule in the Constitution or including them in the list of tribes in the Schedule of Tribes. It did recognize the fact that 'first and probably the most important step in mainstreaming the DNTs is to "recognize" them explicitly. Since the nomenclature of "Denotified" communities came into being in 1952, i.e., two years after the Constitution of India was adopted in 1950, one obvious solution would be to recognize them constitutionally through an amendment'. While the working group noted the almost unanimous opinion in favour of such an amendment in the community leadership, which was echoed in the TAG and Commission reports, it still felt it prudent to reject the same on the ground that it would amount to amending the Constitution of India. So, one then ends with a question, what is to be done?

Speak Up a Revolution

S. Choudhary

A t 12.40 a.m. on 3 July 1972, when Indian Prime Minister Indira Gandhi and President of the Islamic Republic of Pakistan Zulfiqar Ali Bhutto signed the famous Shimla Agreement (the agreement was dated 2 July 1972) in the Indian Institute of Advanced Study at Rashtrapati Niwas, legendary BBC correspondent Mark Tully could not send a voice report because phone lines in Shimla were down that night.

The meeting was held in the backdrop of the 1971 war between India and Pakistan which gave birth to a new nation called Bangladesh. Pakistan, for the first time, gave recognition to Bangladesh that day.

This was a very big international news story that night and it should have been breaking news—according to current media language—but could not get reported.

Things have changed much as far as communication goes. Anyone can now have access to a mobile phone and is also connected to the Internet through Wi-Fi round the clock almost uninterrupted.

But many things have also not changed in the media.

After the last Viceroy went back to Britain in 1947, Indian politics turned democratic. A new Republic of India was born where every citizen has an equal right to vote.

India as a nation has found in the last so many years that though much remains to be desired for a better functioning political democracy, it is much better than aristocracy.

This is the same story from all over the world.

Slowly but steadily, the whole world is moving towards a democratic form of governance. Where there is no democracy, people are fighting in streets and facing bullets demanding the same.

It is now like a universal truth that democracy is a better system to rule oneself.

When policies are formed by participation of more people, it works for the betterment of more people rather than the other way round as happened in aristocracies.

Control by a few generally ends up helping the privileged few.

The twentieth century has been the century of democratization of world politics.

Like politics, communication and media also affects our present and future.

Communication and community, these two words look interrelated: We build a community the way we communicate.

If our communication is not democratic, it is difficult to build a robust democratic community.

We need democratic communication for a better functioning political democracy, but our mass media, till date, remains aristocratic.

Though politics has been democratized, mass media the world over remains top-down and aristocratic in nature.

Though India is basically a rural country with 69 per cent still living in rural areas, the Indian media is urban centric and hardly reports anything about rural lives, apart from crime and disasters.

The news agenda is set by a few in Indian cities, as Viceroys, kings and their chosen ministers earlier decided what was good and bad for most of us.

Earlier news selection was done in a professional manner. But with a definite decline in the institution of editors, news is dictated more and more by vested interests.

Like everywhere, there are honourable exceptions, but the structure of media is such that the interest of the owner community more or less dictates the news selection process.

This has resulted in a topsy-turvy situation where the interests of 70 per cent people have roughly less than 30 per cent space in Indian media and 30 per cent people have more than 70 per cent space.

When issues are not given space, the process of their resolution also does not take place.

When people's issues are neglected due to this faulty system, they are forced to look for other often non-democratic avenues to address their problems.

The Maoist problem in central India seems to be a classic example of the outcome of a non-democratic communication paradigm.

In central India, security forces are fighting a pitched bloody battle with Adivasis (indigenous people) led by Maoist communist guerrillas.

Former Indian Prime Minister Dr Manmohan Singh called it 'India's biggest internal security threat'.

A close inspection finds that the majority of those Adivasis, who are foot soldiers of the Maoist army, are doing so as an alternative to find a solution to their day-to-day problems.

They are there because the Indian mainstream media fails to raise their concerns and in turn, get their issues resolved.

It is an accident of history that Maoist politicians chose Dandakaranya forest in central India as their refuge when they were defeated and were dragged out of Indian cities in the 1970s.

Had the central Indian Adivasis accepted the Islamist jehadi leadership, one could have described the tribal agitators as jehadi.

But in reality, both are examples also of problems of a faulty communication system to a great extent.

Ideally, if we have a democratic communication system where everyone can raise their voices and be heard, many will not have to take the path of violence to solve their problems as they are doing today.

The majority of Maoist supporters are there not because of the attraction of Maoist ideology, but because of the push of the mainstream system, including the media, which does not give appropriate space to their aspirations.

Left or right, extremist views and ideologies will be there in any society, but it only becomes a problem when a large number in the middle become their supporters.

Though the media today only concentrates on extremism on both sides, the real story it seems is in the middle, which it completely fails to recognize.

In places like central India which is the hub of the country's forest and mineral resources, a majority of people want to continue with the forest and agriculture-based economy which is more accommodative of a larger number of people.

The mainstream media, which is controlled by corporate interests in industrial and mining-based economy, deliberately ignores those aspirations and in return, pushes people on the lap of ideologies like Maoism.

But is a democratic and more representative media possible?

My former classmates, some of whom are Maoist foot soldiers now, told me: 'Democratize your communication system and problems like Naxalism will be solved.'

'Make a media like air, a nature-made media, which is not owned by anyone or owned by everyone, where everyone has equal right to raise their issues, tell their stories. Many of these wars will never take place,' they told me.

So, is this a solution?

But how do we make a democratic media which is owned by everyone?

We can try by giving equal ownership of mass media platforms to each of us. But that seems to be as distant a reality as a Maoist revolution is in India.

But some revolutions have already taken place. They are a reality and we must make use of them to try to make a democratic communication platform.

The Internet is a democratic communication platform. An e-listserv is a sort of democratic communication platform like a village panchayat (council) meeting under a banyan tree, if we ignore the issue of where the server which stores these messages is located and who owns it.

So, a few of us started an e-discussion forum in Chhattisgarh to discuss issues which are not covered by the mainstream media. Chhattisgarh is the epicentre of the Maoist movement in central India today.

But Internet penetration is less than 10 per cent in Adivasi areas of central India. So many cannot take part in an e-discussion forum. The Internet is not democratic enough in countries like India.

Less than 40 per cent people have access to good Internet in India.

But unlike the Internet, mobile phones have reached the remotest parts, even in forest areas in central India.

If we can link an e-discussion forum with mobile phones, it can create a democratic communication platform where the last person of society will have an equal voice.

This way, CGNet Swara was born in 2010. It is now accessed by all the Adivasis in the central belt of India: Chhattisgarh, Madhya Pradesh, Odisha, Gujarat, Rajasthan, etc.

CG means Central Gondwana, the central part of that mythical island of Gondwana which included Asia, Africa and Australia where Adivasis or original inhabitants started their journey.

Swara means voice in Sanskrit.

If you add voice to the Internet, you can create a flat communication platform even in places like central India where the majority own a phone but not a computer.

An Inequitable Communication System

Listening to reports on www.cgnetswara.org is an extraordinary experience. They are from people who sound as rustic as their stories do. The use of dialects is common and sometimes the language is one that is known only to a tribal community.

It is the first time perfectly ordinary people are deciding what news is and how to say it. They do not know another media that will tell their stories. Often, they do not know how their telephone calls result in action. They just call on a phone number they have been given by a user.

On 27 March 2012, one Anil Bamne reported on Swara that the government-subsidized rice for mid-day meals in primary schools had not been supplied for five months. The children belonged to the displaced families from tribal areas in Chhattisgarh. Priyanka Netam in Mumbai in the western Indian state of Maharashtra, thousands of kilometres away, who knew neither Anil nor the village, was moved by the plight of the children. She called the responsible minister in Raipur. Not surprisingly, the minister was more curious about how Priyanka knew about this school in a remote area of Chhattisgarh, a state which is still not known to many outsiders. The minister tried to explain that the village was hard to reach, even for the government. Priyanka felt the minister was trying to wash her hands of the issue but Priyanka did not give up. Seeing her persistence, the minister offered to suspend the officer concerned. Priyanka argued that this would not address the real problem of providing nutritional meals for the children. At the end of some long and rather painful exchanges, Priyanka recorded on CGNet Swara on 12 April, that twelve quintals of rice had been delivered and mid-day meals were restarted.

On 11 November 2013, Khuturam Sunani reported that a twelve-year-old schoolgirl in Chhattisgarh had been allegedly molested by her headmaster. A report had been lodged by the parents ten days ago, but the headmaster had not been arrested.

In his message, Khuturam also gave the numbers of the police officer in-charge. Right after the news was posted, many indignant listeners called up the Superintendent of Police and the District Magistrate, the people in charge. Within three days, the headmaster was arrested.

Afzal Khan's report about a bank in Bhopalpatnam, Chhattisgarh helped the local tendu patta labour to get their money. Tendu patta is the leaf of a plant and is collected by the locals from the forest for rolling a type of cigarette called beedi. This is the main earning for the poor who depend on forest produce for their livelihood. They had been paid by cheque and the local bank refused to pay out the money, saying there were old unpaid loans in the name of their family members. Afzal also provided the listeners the phone number of the bank officials who heard from a lot of people. The reaction was immediate, with special counters set up to reimburse the money.

On CGNet Swara, the stories seem to repeat themselves; they are just from different parts of the country. Apparently, the concerns the poor face in most parts of India are also repetitive. The inadequate performance of village schoolteachers is common. In proportion to the number of children, there are not enough of them appointed. Very often they live in a nearby town instead of the village the school is in. Traveling daily by an uncertain transport system, they are unable to maintain regularity and the children waste time waiting. Even though their salaries are for the work of teaching, they are roped into other government welfare schemes, for example immunization or election duty. This distracts the teacher. In some places, teachers have been known to even subcontract work to local, less qualified people. The concern displayed in the messages is touching. Often parents who have themselves never gone to school, speak of how their child who does not get a teacher will never have a chance to make his life better.

Non-payment of wages in the government employment guarantee scheme is another recurring theme. The MGNREGA is a much-flaunted government promise. Although the government assures 100 days of labour and payment within fifteen days, people have had to wait for years, initially for sanction of work and then for payment.

Sometimes, work records are fudged by corrupt members of the village council. So, people are using the message board to record these deviations. New links are being formed.

The bonding between people in the same boat shows up in Pitbasu Bhoi's poignant story.

He was on the hundredth day of his MGNREGA work in Chhattisgarh and had not been paid when Rakesh Kumar helped him record his plight on Swara. After a few days, Sanjay Madhav Seth, who had heard the report on Swara, happened to meet someone in a hospital. This man's son was ill and he needed money urgently. When the man confided that his MGNREGA dues had not been settled, Sanjay asked him if it was his story on Swara. Indeed, it was Pitbasu. So, Sanjay recorded another message. In the meantime, Pitbasu lost his son, but the message was heard by some activists and they took up the matter strongly. Mainstream newspapers picked up the news. Pitbasu's payment still did not come easily. The officers in charge tried to push the matter under the carpet, which was again reported on Swara. Finally, the money was paid and now Pitbasu, an unassuming villager, is helping other people use CGNet Swara. It is not surprising that his interviews compete with those done by professional journalists. He is in his element because he is speaking his heart out. Clearly that does not require too much media training.

Although helplines with toll-free numbers are common, they are the conventional pleading-based systems where the process is not transparent. The officer who can solve the problem is all-powerful. It simply provides a possibility to keep an accurate record and can work in a system that guarantees uniformity of reach and efficiency of management. But when the complainant is someone with little sense of empowerment, the impact is likely to be feeble. And where would a person go if the helpline does not yield aid? The attempt to reach someone higher up also needs to be made through the same route and the disempowered find themselves crushed.

'The officers are also changing in their treatment,' says Chandrakant in Kabirdham district of Chhattisgarh. 'When we used to meet them earlier, they would not listen carefully. We had to make many visits to their office and wait for their attention. Now they tell us that we should go to them first and not report every small problem on CGNet Swara,' he added.

Some government officials are happy to use the messages as feedback and have got involved to take corrective action. 'It gives me a finger on the pulse of the people,' said one official.

The impact on the person who hears from an officer is huge. Rajim was overwhelmed when she got a phone call from the state's chief secretary. 'I am nobody,' she says, 'He called me and explained what I can do and he has promised to take action. He encouraged me and said I should go on helping the people'.

What will she do if no action is taken?

'I will leave another message on CGNet Swara. I know now that the highest officers are listening to us,' she says. It is hard to be sceptical in the face of her enthusiasm.

Sharing experiences also helps. Listening to the way one person solved his problem has shown many other users the same path.

Hem Singh Markam is a tribal who lives in a small village called Sajankhar. 'Ten years back we were told by the government to move here from the forest on the mountains where we lived. I prepared this land by my own hands for cultivation. The government promised us ownership with proper papers, but nothing has moved,' he said. The village has no electricity and the source of water was three kilometres away. With other villagers, Markam made innumerable applications and visits to the village council and the Public Health Engineering Department, requesting

that the village be given at least a hand pump for water. The last
three years were very frustrating and his first message on CGNet
Swara reflected his anger with the government not keeping the
promises made.

He could see that others were recording the phone numbers
of the people who could actually solve the problem. So, he
was encouraged to find the telephone numbers of the officials
responsible for his hand pump and record them in his message.
Within a month, two hand pumps were dug in his village.

Now he is convinced that the Internet is a powerful tool. 'I do
not know what the Internet is, and I cannot explain it to you, but I
will say that you should try it like I did, and see for yourself. There
is no need to feel hopeless. This works,' he says to others.

Swara means voice and CGNet Swara, the voice of Central
Gondwana was launched in February 2010 with the tribals of
central India at its core. It is the brainchild of Shubhranshu, a
veteran journalist. He has worked earlier with The Guardian and
the BBC.

'There are hardly any tribal journalists and the others do not
understand their language,' he says. 'When I travelled to other
countries in my work with the BBC, I used to take the help of local
journalists for translation. But working in tribal areas I realized that
here there are no tribal journalists or journalists who understand
the tribal languages. Secondly the lives of the tribals and the urban
journalist are so different that the context is hard to appreciate,' he
added.

What gets conveyed, even by well-meaning urban journalists,
as the opinion of the tribal is often skewed, as it is being transmitted
through a select Hindi- or English-speaking minority, which
conveys tribal concerns to the outside world.

Education is often cited as the ultimate remedy for all problems
by the educated middle class and the well-meaning urbanite. But
the reality is that education is not coming to the people in a way
that they can make use of it. It is not delivering what it promises

to. In more than seven decades after Independence, the reality of literacy in tribal areas is pathetic. Where they have been taught to sign their names, they are often not able to read or grasp the impact of the written word.

'Poor people in general, and tribals especially, are oral communities. The educated class has focused on writing. But the majority of people are more comfortable speaking and listening rather than reading or writing,' says Shubhranshu.

Tribals in central India, like many other original people elsewhere in the world, have a very strong oral tradition and in India there are 100 million of them. When India was divided into states after it attained Independence, boundaries were drawn mainly on the basis of the language spoken in an area. Though many tribals shared a language and a culture, they were separated from each other by state boundaries. For example, Gondi is spoken by tribals in the central Indian belt that runs through states like Chhattisgarh, Madhya Pradesh, Maharashtra, Odisha, Telangana and Andhra Pradesh. The schools in each of these states have chosen their particular languages as the medium of instruction. The few Gondi-speaking people who went to school studied from different state schools. These, the educated tribals, forgot their mother tongue. They have made some progress as individuals but have lost the ability to talk to each other. Their community has been divided.

The tribal languages are not recognized by the government and gradually those who speak their own language are being limited to their homes or close communities. For example, in some tribal villages, the people have absolutely no way of connecting with the outside world, because they speak only their own language and have not had access to even primary education in their mother tongue, though the Constitution promises it.

Shubhranshu had set up an online discussion group called CGNet in 2004. It was intended to be a platform for concerned citizens to exchange views on issues related to central India. Although he felt strongly that radio would be the best medium for the region, the laws did not allow the community radio movement to grow. At least the Internet was affordable, though its reach was suspect. 'In India, so many people do not have reliable electricity, and in their lifetime it is unlikely that they will acquire it, or be able to ever afford a computer, or use it. Computers are expensive, and literacy is abysmal,' he says.

Over the following years, he roped in many volunteers on the ground. The Internet group and a people's website could help reach their news to the global media. Someone would call CGNet on the telephone to report happenings which they would put out in the network through the discussion group or telephone calls to individuals. Gradually, more and more of the messages could be verified by others on the ground. And CGNet developed as a hub for information about the area. Usually, the news is first taken up by local media. The national and global media follow next. But this has been reversed in the case of Chhattisgarh, by the use of this bottom-up media.

In the last decade, having access to modern technology has been empowering Indians. Social media is being used by people to raise concerns, just as it has happened in other parts of the world. The number of phone users has jumped up in the last decade. More than two-thirds of Indians have mobile phones. In rural areas, even in relatively poor communities, phone connections were growing.

In Sunnamatka in Andhra Pradesh, the villagers walk eight kilometres for water and there is no electricity to charge the phone locally. But there are six mobile phones in use. They are charged at the time of the visit to the weekly market.

'The network is not great. Nagendra would call me from a treetop and I could only leave text messages for him to call me, because I knew he would get them when he was in the network range,' says Shubhranshu. 'I was looking for a way to connect the phone calls to the Internet group. I was lucky to find a connection to a group of students who were working on a project using phones in the computer science department of Massachusetts Institute of

Technology. They helped me get the first model of Swara. This simple technological intervention has changed things dramatically. At CGNet Swara, when you call the phone number you hear a voice which asks you to make a simple choice: press one to record and two to listen. This is called an interactive voice recorder (IVR) system. The messages come to the website where they can be edited and posted with text, audio and picture. The criteria for releasing messages is quite simple: it should be true, impacting lives in the community, and not abusive. The subject of the reports is chosen by the people who call in.'

A phone user calling the telephone number gets to listen to the latest messages, just as the web user can find them all on the website at any time, like blog posts.

This simple process has worked as a bridge between the two kinds of people: the ones who have web access and those who don't. The network of users has grown mostly by word of mouth.

Some formal training and workshops have been conducted. The participants were carefully chosen from among the grassroots organizations already in the e-discussion group. These were mostly struggling rural activists who had no place to share their concerns. The mainstream media ignored them almost totally. They quickly grasped the power that could be available to them and the people with whom they worked.

Two cultural teams of CGNet volunteers are also on the road, visiting villages and Adivasi haats (weekly markets) every day. They sing, dance and do puppet shows to teach them how to use their mobile phones and to tell the world about the world around them.

Once people had learnt how to use CGNet Swara, they in turn trained many others to use the number effectively. The platform has an appeal for the people because it is simple to use. It is causing the change that people want in their lives, after they share their problem. They are able to build public opinion around the issues that matter to them.

By connecting with the mainstream media, CGNet has tried to get a wide coverage for issues. This has been especially effective in conflict areas where media access was restricted. The lack of communication with the world, including the government and the media had turned Chhattisgarh into the 'biggest internal security threat' for the country, in the words of Dr Singh.

A neutral, peace-loving people were forced to take sides in a conflict between ultra-left, extremist Maoists and government security forces. To add to their plight, government-supported vigilante group Salwa Judum acquired power and weapons to wreak havoc and violence on the common man. Thousands died, their homes were burnt, their crops destroyed and they were forced to flee to the roadside and live in camps. But the world did not know what was happening there and why.

Industrial interests impact the media in a way that is detrimental to the poor. Often media houses are owned and run by the same people who have vested interests directly in economic growth, which requires such violent strategies harming the majority of people. And anyway, the market drives the news indirectly. After all, a newspaper which costs many times the sale price to print is dependent on advertisement revenue.

This was happening in Chhattisgarh where the CGNet community claims to have prevented this genocide by bringing out the news of the security forces, the vigilante group and the Maoists, when local mainstream media could not fulfil its responsibility.

Naturally, the issue of credibility needs special care.

From 11 March 2011 onwards, there were telephone calls to CGNet Swara, over tribal homes being burnt in village after village in a 15-kilometre radius around Tadmetla. A year before, on 5 April 2010, 76 members of the security force had been killed in an attack by the Maoists in Tadmetla.

'It was a difficult decision whether or not to make these messages public, as there was no way to verify them. The people who were calling had only heard of the news, there was no one who had actually been there and seen it happen,' says Shubhranshu. 'In the middle of all the violence, who would call us? Who would risk being identified? Finally when we got the same news from many different people, we asked someone on our network who was in a safe place, to send out a request to the media to explore the issue.'

Two stories that appeared in two national newspapers, *The Hindu* and the *Times of India*, would not have been possible without these citizen reports. They are hair-raising accounts of the devastation wreaked on hapless tribals. Both reports speak of the journalists being prevented from visiting the area.

Journalists, however, are beginning to take note of the problems around free speech. There is a growing respect and acceptance for news produced by ordinary citizens, even though the presentation may be of poor quality. CGNet Swara receives an average of 500 calls a day from people accessing those reports on their phones.

What has moved the web users to participate in the lives of people that they have never known? No formal research has been carried out yet, but it is probably the stronger connection that is made by listening to people tell their story. What can sound sterile in words written by one person on behalf of another, is alive in the actual recording from a real person. Add a phone number to that, and credibility goes up many times. A reporter in the mainstream media or a bureaucrat whose area is being spoken about can just pick up his phone and talk to check.[1]

First the written word and then picture and video, have been given lots of importance the world over. The oral form of communication has been downplayed. In places like India, oral communication is suppressed to the level of being criminalized. Radio news on private channels is still banned and government-owned radio is the only source of information for a huge number of people living in remote villages.

Mainstream political parties and people's movements in India too have ignored the oral form of mass communication and have depended heavily on written forms. It is hardly surprising that the masses remain largely alienated and people's participation in the democratic process itself is low.

Illiterates are not seen as potential by market forces, as we do not see much research on audio communication to make it more manageable. Knowledge on the Internet is mostly created by people. By leaving out so many people, knowledge itself is being limited.

As Shubhranshu points out, 'In places like central India more than 70 per cent people are on the wrong side of digital divide and their knowledge is not mainstream because of this last mile disconnect. In India not more than 40 per cent have access to the Internet. By linking mobile to computer we can make the knowledge of the majority mainstream. Then our entire world will be richer with this huge inflow of oral knowledge.'

There is a charge in his voice as his imagination speeds ahead: 'And imagine what we could do if we could search by speaking! It would be a revolution like the world has not seen. Like democracy, voice is also chaotic. Technology needs to help make it manageable. Our politics has democratized, but our mass communication platforms still remain aristocratic. This needs to change. Swara is a small experiment in that direction.'

Voice might well be the next technological revolution that is needed in the world.

A poor man's Google, a poor man's Facebook and an audio newspaper where they themselves report?

Like politics, journalism should also become everybody's business.

Maybe it is a paradigm shift in the making.

Recommendations

1. Like politics, the media should be democratized. Each has a vote, similarly each voice should have similar importance.

With the advent of the Internet and mobile phones, this looks a real possibility.

2. Social media should not be restricted to only the Internet. It should also include people who feel more comfortable speaking than writing. It needs to be a place for responsible communication.

3. Radio should be opened up immediately and news should also be allowed in radio. Community Radio should have similar freedom as commercial ones.

4. Democracy should move towards digital democracy with an all-encompassing digital platform where all can be connected through the Internet, phone, Bluetooth, etc., but should not be a tool for monitoring.

Indigenous Republic (Indigenocracy)

Ghanshyam

The democracy that has evolved in the last 250–300 years in Western civilization is now an established parameter for the whole world. It gives prime importance to individuals and their freedom.

Democracy is made up of two words, 'demos' and 'cracy'. 'Demos' means people and 'cracy' means system; it can also be termed as a system of people. This has been internalized in Hindi as 'Loktantra'. Western democracy is a system developed from capitalism, which puts individual capital, individual autonomy and individual rights at the centre. Thus, today's democracy is a system evolved from a capitalist system which provides prime importance to the individual and capital.

In contrast to these ideals of capital, individual and inequality, the indigenous republic establishes the idea of community, labour and equality. The indigenous republic flourishes in a community built on the ideals of variety, difference and tolerance. Thus, it is not only a political system, but a collective social, cultural, economic and justice system. This incorporates individual freedom as well as the importance of family. In this conception, the individual is free, but is a living unit of a society governed by the importance of family.

The indigenous republic is a political system based on an economic republic in which the government, administration and justice structures are autonomous and shaped by societal morality, familial needs and the individual's disciplined wish. In this system, a corrupt government cannot obliterate or swallow society. Neither can society curb individual freedom nor can an individual victimize society by being undisciplined and opting for a materialist nature. The indigenous republic, in a sense, is a republic system based on principles of justice, unity, secularism and equality in which governance of society, family's autonomy and self-reliance and person's self-respect is incorporated. It is a global community system free of race, gender and caste discrimination and a society which is governed by differences and specialties. The indigenous republic can morph into an easy-going, compassionate system free from fear, hunger and terror. In such a system, a person can live with humanity, a society can progress with respect and the government can preserve human pride with compassion. In the words of the poet Badrinarayan:

I am the innumerable instrument of the season's hands
I am the infinite cry on Twitter
I am the immeasurable sound of Earth wings
I am the primal mating of human and soil.

Tribal Existence (Community's Existence)

The indigenous republic is another name for community republic. In a community republic, the possibility to strengthen the existence, tradition, lifestyle, skills and the innate capabilities of a community's people is present. To elaborate, the following points must be kept in mind: self-dependence, self-governance, self-respect, production ability and communality.

Self-Dependence

There are parameters of self-dependence which society has developed through nature, mind and tradition. They are food, clothes, education, home, health, entertainment and exchange.

Food

Apart from grains, vegetables, fruits, fish and dairy products, fuel, water and utensils are the basic necessities. All of these have been developed by human beings based on natural resources and geographical specialties. Thus, cuisines are varied. People dwelling in forests have used fruits and vegetables procured from forests and meat from wild animals as their food sources. Similarly, people from deserts have made foods and drinks based on their natural availability. Those dwelling in plains depend on grains, especially rice and wheat and people residing on the coast have feasted on sea food.

The indigenous republic has developed a system based on their skills and experience with regard to food, clothing, health, education, shelter, entertainment and exchange. It has similarly developed various methods and resources for crop production, domesticating animals, drinking, bathing and washing on the basis of water availability. People developed wells, tube wells, ponds and tanks on the basis of their geo-natural specifications and at some places, they made use of rivers and seas.

Human society has always endeavoured to minimize fuel consumption in cooking based on their needs, habits and natural conditions. The tendency to cook only once a day during summers is observed in many regions. Leftovers are soaked in water overnight and the fermented food, known as 'paanata' or 'pakhaal bhaat', is had the next morning. This can be observed in states like Bihar, West Bengal, Odisha, Jharkhand and Chhattisgarh. Availability of fuel is dependent on forest and animals. In this regard, we can say that food is directly related to the soil, forest and animals. Food and water are dependent on usability and availability of land and forest.

These communities have thoughtfully developed skills, techniques and methods of using these resources bestowed on us by nature in a governed manner. Jharkhand's farmers often reply 'kheti-baari' (farming-foresting) without much thought when asked of their occupation. This is a common phrase, but farming-foresting is a complementary production system. Normally, fields, using irrigation systems, are used to grow grains such as maize, wheat, rice, pulses and oil seeds. Forests produce other necessary proteins, medicines and vitamins through the fruits, vegetables and spices that grow there. Therefore, the farmers and workers of Jharkhand consider forests as an essential part of their lives along with their farms. They have developed this system of self-dependence of food and life from the knowledge and science gained through experience. This can be observed in thousands of villages of Jharkhand even now. Indigenous republicans have also developed their food patterns keeping seasons in mind. This indigenous food tradition is an essential part of the indigenous republic and develops a strong process of economic self-dependence.

Clothes

Human development led to the adoption of various cultural habits in which clothing was an essential step. In ancient times, people used animal skin and leaves to cover themselves. Later, when permanent and temporary shelter systems came into use, women started making clothes from various natural resources such as jute, cotton and wool. These natural resources led to threads, which were used to weave clothes. Thus, the production system of clothes required trees, plants and animals for raw materials. These resources were obtained from forests, animal domestication and farming. This was an important turn in the history of human evolution which linked cultures and nature. Indigenous communities developed clothes according to weather and geo-spatial conditions.

Shelter

Humans developed shelters for the purpose of domesticating animals, securing lives, safety from weather conditions, reproduction and copulation. In this, women had central importance. According to the specifications of the natural surroundings, geographical conditions and to preserve life and make it comfortable, women made clothes and developed astrological skills that gave shape to homes. Indigenous communities established homes in the form of a relationship between nature and humans.

Indigenous communities have always taken resources from nature for their homes. Soil for walls, bamboo for roof, leaves for cots, etc. This can be easily understood by looking at houses of Jharkhand's societies. In the art inscribed on their walls using natural colours, their relationship with nature can also be observed. The liveliness of life in Jharkhand is told in its walls: their work patterns, music and the colours of life.

Health

The indigenous community of Jharkhand normally considers a person's health on the mental, physical and sense fronts. Jharkhand's community divides health into two categories: safety and precaution and cures. This community focuses on safety to lessen the chances of anyone, either animals or humans, falling ill. The immune system is developed and sports, nutritious food, dance and cleanliness are emphasized. Nutritious and wholesome food with medical benefits is taken from nature and mostly consumed raw and in a seasonal cycle. Food is only cooked if required from a health perspective.

The community doesn't use those vegetables or other substances growing in particular seasons that are unsuitable from a health point of view. For instance, pumpkins are not used in poos (October) and leafy vegetables in savan-bhado (July-August). For safety from a health perspective, they also complement organic food in specific seasons with different types of meat. In the monsoons, for instance, different types of mushrooms, snails, rats, insects, frogs, snake, fish and ants are consumed without hesitation.

They also save themselves from mental strain by organizing different types of community sports, singing and dance. This results in a healthy person and strong communities. In this way, man and community establish a tuned relationship with nature and strengthen the process of health safety.

If they fall ill, they use medicines, vegetables and leaves to treat people from the knowledge acquired through experience. Usually, each family has enough knowledge to treat simple ailments. They go to see a doctor in case of specific ailments. The vaidya (doctor) first focuses on the fever, pulse rates and taste buds of the ill person.

Entertainment

The tribal community does not see entertainment as exhibition. Art and culture are embedded in their lives as veins in our body. In tribal life, every activity from birth to death takes the form of art and culture. Nature, design and culture are multi-dimensional specialties of entertainment.

In the culture and entertainment system of Jharkhand, Khovar and Sohrai art has a special contribution. Sculpted images inscribed on the walls, rocks and caves of Jharkhand show the liveliness of their art and entertainment. The observer of Manjusha folk art and tribal folk art, Shekhar Roy, says Khovar and Sohrai art is primarily related to reproduction and grain production. Khovar is related to their marriage system and entertainment and Sohrai is associated with farming and domestication of animals. Khovar or Khobar literally means a married couple inside a cave. At wedding ceremonies, designs on soil are created by women. Some of the visuals are community specific; for instance, Munda houses show rainbows, snakes floating in air, flowers and symbols of ancestors. Sohrai art is basically created in October–November during the time of the harvest festival. The designs are created on the walls after the polishing and renovation of houses. Sohrai art depicts many human designs, air-floating snakes, giant horses, deer, oxen, peacocks, flowers, plants and other geometric designs.

Similarly, in dance and singing, on one side there lies an ocean-like expanse of maize fields and on the other side, there is a serene river stream. The lyrics sung possess the profound tranquility of forests and the wide expanse of the sky.

Singing and dancing have no audience and no age bar. The love songs sung set the hearts of the singing and dancing folk free of inhibitions and constraints, bringing freedom with the words and tunes sung.

Exchange

Tribal communities don't believe in loans and interest and profits. This society believes in co-operation and bartering. These systems provide the market a humanitarian face. Here, the market is not only a place to buy and sell, but a place of human gathering. People dress up before going to the market by using marigold and other available flowers. Thus, the market is a place of enjoyment and dialogue between people.

The exchange system opens the gate of co-ownership over life-sustaining substances produced by society rather than keeping them in stores. This process governs human relations as well as the man-nature relationship.

In processes of production and reproduction, this system of exchange is simple and natural. Land is no object, women aren't objects of pleasure and markets aren't places to buy and sell.

Self-Governance

Systems of administration have been a matter of debate worldwide. In today's world, democracy is considered a good governance system. The flow from autocracy to democracy has been going on through various modes for thousands of years. Sometimes, the system crushes its people and the ruling class goes unchecked and uses the system for its whims. This age of global power and global economy has made democracy dishonest. Democracy as a political system has been under severe stress in the West and in other parts of the world; but it is true that western democracies have often subjugated other nations in the past.

In this age of hopelessness, it is necessary that we ponder over a new system which makes democracy work for the people, communities and nature.

Indigenocracy is one such philosophy. The indigenous republic puts prime importance on self-governance. Any ruling method can become good governance only when the system is self-governed or community-governed. In this aspect, indigenocracy is a system of the community, by the community and for the community. Since nature is filled with variety and differences, no one central system of governance can fulfil the needs and dreams of everyone. Thus, we must keep the unit of governance so small that each member of the community can make the system work for their dreams, aspirations and needs. There should be a spiral relationship between the largest and smallest unit of governance, like concentric circles. In this spiral governance system, there won't only be place for human beings, but also for the river's songs, the waterfall's thumping, nature's progress and animals' well-being. This system would allow each individual to share their part of happiness and carry another's grief. There would be no ruler and no ruled. Consequently, a time will come when state power would diminish and there would be free meeting of humans and a symbiotic relationship with nature would be established.

In this way, the self-governing system would establish such a political process which would take the form from a localized body to a globalized one. Locality, nationality and globality would be interconnected, despite being standalone political units. It would be similar to the root, stem and leaves on a tree. All have their independent existence but are complementary to each other.

Similarly, in a community republic system, the community works as root, the nation-state as stem and global order as the leaves. Thus, community, nation-state and global order are interconnected. The community republic system is a global self-governing system where politics, economics and sociology are complementary to each other.

Producibility

In a self-governed republic, special emphasis has always been on developing the innate capability and producibility of humans. It values human labour and animal labour in the same way. Labour is not for sale.

Thus, producibility imbibes these points: dedication towards labour, respect for skill, sharing of labour and development of technology.

Self-Respect

The indigenous republic has been adamant in preserving the self-respect of human beings. History is evidence to the fact that whenever the self-respect of humans had been hurt by an external force, the community has revolted as one. Since self-respect is an essential condition of being human, the indigenous republic places special focus on preserving and honouring self-respect.

Communality

Community life was developed on the principle of kutumbakam (community as a home). Entire communities have developed, flourished and been strengthened on this principle. Kutumbakam is a community lifestyle based on multi-dimensional human relationships. In order to appreciate the 'kutumbakam community', one need to give up the established historiography depicting history as a progression of the relationship between the dominator and the dominated. it would be necessary to view history as an expression of the ordinary people, the oppressed and the Dalits. From this perspective, all history is a process of consolidation of the geo-cultural and geo-seasonal contexts. In other words, such a history will place human advent in the larger context of natural evolution extending beyond the life and memory of humans. Placing humans in the context of environment can bring us closer to the historical truth of how societies have evolved over millennia.

Community Method for Indigenous Water Conservation

Water has played a prime role in human evolution and development. Most civilizations have flourished near water sources. Cultures have come into being through the pure flow of seas, rivers, ponds and lakes. Over thousands of years, communities, with knowledge acquired through experience, have invented various techniques to conserve water. In this aspect, the tribal community is more affluent and developed than other communities.

The tribal communities of Jharkhand have developed various methods of water conservation from ponds, lakes, pokhars, pans, dobha, wells and raw dams.

In Santhal Pargana and Chotanagpur, thousands of aahars (watersheds) and small dams can be observed even today, even if in their tattered state. All these conservatory methods had been largely done by the tribal communities of Jharkhand.

The irrigation and canal commissions established in 1901-1903 have accepted the truth that these regions (Chotanagpur and Santhal Pargana) had proper conservation methods to sustain them during droughts, particularly by conserving rainwater in their aahars. When the commission asked the working commissioner F.A. Slack if the number of aahars should be increased, he replied in the affirmative.[1]

The farmers of this region had started farming practices by keeping in mind the usability of the system of perforation of water in jungle lands, the manure from animal dung and the leaves, herbs and shrubs of the region. There are many crops like paddy, maize, corn and barley which grow in less water and can also digest large amount of water. Farmers understood the natural and environmental condition and thus developed modern water conservation methods through shapes of farming lands, irrigation systems and techniques of farming, useful seeds and the use of manure and pesticides.

Shapes of Farming Lands

This can be understood by observing lands of Chotanagpur and Santhal Pargana that have different shapes than the farming lands of plains. Usually, these lands are bound though skewed linhays. The height of linhays on slopes are higher. Farmers made them according to water flow and shapes of lands. They introduced the system of sucking out extra water. In today's scientific terms, they had developed contour trenches.

The construction of linhays is done by farmers to restrain the need for water, protect the soil and collect leaves in their lands. Usually, these are wide and have a height of around 1–1.5 feet. According to their needs, farmers change their dimensions. The difference in their structure can be observed through slopes of these lands. Grass grows on linhays and makes it permanent. On big linhays, plants which grow faster are planted. And at some places, slow growing plants are planted such as pine, palaash and jaamun tree.

Irrigation System for Farming Lands

Many complete irrigation systems are adapted in these regions to irrigate lands. This involves construction of raw dams, making pits around the slopes to collect rainwater and construction of aahars and ponds for bigger slopes.

Raw dams are constructed usually at two places. First, temporary dams at natural water sources are often constructed in the months of November and December after the rains. Crops grown after the paddy harvest are irrigated through them. These are also used for purposes of washing and bathing and by animals. These dams wash out during the rainy season.

The height of these dams is made according to the needs of farmers and an opening is made for excess water to flow out. The width and height of such dams are usually three-five feet. The width is decided according to the stream flow velocity of the water.

Apart from this, dams of soil are made near the centre of the slope to collect the water flowing through these slopes. The length, breadth and height of these are decided according to the quantity of water flowing in. The linhays of these dams are planted with trees whose leaves turn into useful manure. All the trees are planted in that region of slope from where the leaves fall into the crop field. Usually there are big farming lands on the lower part of these dams. Water from this place is used when there is no rainfall or when there is shortage of it.

Ponds

Ponds have an old history. Farmers here use water collected over more than fifty years. Ponds and lakes are mentioned in texts such as the *Ain-i-Akbari*, *Ramcharitmanas* and Mahabharata. The British have referred to them as well.

Reports given to Irrigation Department (1901–03) by Jarid mentioned, 'Though the possibility of the irrigation of this land is very less, but whatever is left has been done to 90 per cent by these ponds.' The reality of the reports of 1901–03 can be found in the documents of 1962–61. Out of 1,49,606 acres of land, 95,376 acres has been irrigated by these ponds.

It is clear from the above-mentioned documents that the irrigation system of Chotanagpur and Santhal Pargana was through ponds. Ponds are different from dams and are closed from three to four ends. By closing the pond from three ends, one end is left from where rainwater flows in. When the ponds are closed on all sides, channels are created for allowing inflow of water. Similarly, outlets are provided for taking care of water if it overflows the bunds. On all sides of the ponds, trees are planted to absorb the overflowing water. At the linhay of ponds, big trees and shrubs are planted.

Construction of Pit Holes and Wells

The practice of irrigation of crops through pit holes and wells has existed in these areas for a long time. At a corner of the crop field, pit holes five-seven feet in diameter are made. At some places, they are either formed in circular or square shapes. Wells are generally in circular shapes. The depth of these pit holes is from ten to fifteen feet. The opening of the well can be of six inches to one foot from the level of ground. This method is as old as that of the ponds. Nearly a little over a quarter of the land area is under irrigation provided through these pit holes.

Selection of Seeds Requiring Less Water for Farming

The farmers of Chotanagpur and Santhal Pargana have been selecting beneficial seeds for farming from an earlier age based on their experience and the requirements of the soil. The farmers have knowledge of which crops should be planted in upper and lower fields. Before the planting of seeds, farmers are well aware of how many times ploughing and levelling of field is required and are aware till date. In this process, less water is required.

The upper field, which in their language is known as Bari or Tant, is classified into two sub-categories. Bari is more fertile compared to Tant. Crops used in Tant fields are kurthi, gondli, moong, ghangra, barbatti, madua, shama, kundo, etc., while the main crops for Bari are corn, bajra, chilli, tomato, green vegetables, pulses, kudrum, etc.

Lower fields are classified into two sub-categories: the upper section is known as baad and lower fields are known as gehra or jola. For a baad field, a different type of paddy is used that requires less water and grows in less time than usual. For a gehra field, those seeds are used which don't decay in excessive water. The height of the plants of such paddy is greater than that of upper field.

Traditional seeds of these places have the unique ability to withstand the ups and downs of environment. Pests are rarely seen here and if found, the solution is herbs from the forest or the ashes of leaves.

Techniques for Cropping and Irrigation

In Chotanagpur and Santhal Pargana, the structure of fields is such that tractors were never found useful. Hence for agriculture here, knowledge of techniques from the primitive age is essential.

It is well known by the farmer that the place where they can use a spud and hoe, it is not beneficial to use bulls for ploughing. This discipline of agriculture has taught the farmers how to be brave enough to face harsh days. Even while prime agricultural land in Jharkhand and West Bengal faced drought, people here were little affected. The traditional technique of water harvesting also made farmers overcome the drought.

The farmers know techniques to fetch water from pit holes and wells. To fetch water from wells, water containers such as *sain* are used. Sain requires two people to fetch water while *lattha* and *kundi* require only one person to fetch water. At some places to fetch water, new techniques are used like *rehat*. To keep the water level in check, different techniques for regulation are used as per the region.

Hundreds of such traditional systems are still practised in Jharkhand. Still, work is in progress on these techniques. If work is done on such techniques of water harvesting, all water-related issues would follow the same pattern.

Tribal livelihood depends mostly on agriculture in small land holdings. Adequate irrigation, therefore, is the very lifeline for them. Yet, paucity of irrigation has kept tribal communities in Jharkhand marooned in poverty and deprivation. The development plans given to them by the government have normally overlooked traditional irrigation methods that exist in the area. If they were revived, encouraged and further developed, the entire population stands to benefit. Despite this possibility, the economic condition of the tribal communities in Jharkhand has remained far from satisfactory. Let us hope that tribal knowledge in this field will one day gain the respectability it deserves.

How Not to Manage 'Tribal Affairs'

Abhay Flavian Xaxa

The NDA-II government is about to finish its term and stocktaking is warranted, especially from the Adivasi perspective. The BJP manifesto of the 2014 general elections had clearly committed to the guiding principles of Samajik Nyay (Social Justice) and Samajik Samrasta (Social Harmony) while dealing with tribal affairs of the country. The party had promised to bridge the development deficit between Adivasis and the rest of the population by 'creating an enabling ecosystem of equal opportunity' and furthering economic justice and political empowerment as per the Constitution.

But overall, the Adivasi experience in the subsequent four years has been disappointing, disempowering and disillusioned. The promise of social justice and harmony has only remained rhetorical and tokenistic just like that of all previous political parties in power. In these four years, the number of Adivasi under-trials in jail in Left-Wing Extremism (LWE) areas have only increased, while Adivasi women have been sexually assaulted and tortured with impunity. Various constitutional provisions and safeguards are undermined while the rule of the law is seriously compromised to the extent that Supreme Court orders are openly disregarded.

The much-vaunted attempt of undoing the historical injustice to Adivasis in the form of the Forest Rights Act, 2006 by recognizing individual and community rights has failed due to relentless land grabbing by mining companies. Various provisions of the PESA have continued to be systematically diluted, pushing the Adivasi communities to the margins. The saga of denying development rights to the Adivasis year after year continues in the form of under-allocation, notional allocations, under-spending and non-transparency in the Tribal Sub Plan.

The MMDR Amendment Act, which was passed by the NDA government in 2015, is another attempt towards displacing Adivasis from their traditional land by undermining consent of the communities and environmental regulations. The NDA-II government has displayed serious disregard towards various constitutional authorities like the Supreme Court, Scheduled Tribe Commission, MoTA, TACs, etc., apart from various legal provisions related to protection and development of Adivasis, resulting in continued disempowerment and marginalization of Adivasis across the country.

Token Approach towards Adivasi Rights

Although the NDA-II government made several policy announcements from the Adivasi perspective, most of the government initiatives have been tokenistic and disillusioning. Firstly, a National Tribal Advisory Council with the Prime Minister as its chairman was constituted in 2015 as a nodal body to plan and monitor tribal development schemes. This decision seriously undermines the constitutional status of Tribal Advisory Councils in the states as well as the Governor's position and its overlapping mandate with the NCST. Another major programme announced was the 'Stand-up India' scheme to promote Adivasi entrepreneurs in business ventures. Although the idea is reasonable, it also reminds us of the Prime Minister's pet project, the 'Vanbandhu' scheme, which was announced in 2014 with an allocation of Rs 200 crore and has since disappeared without trace. The three tribal universities set up in Madhya Pradesh, Andhra Pradesh and Telangana have been starved of human and financial resources. Similarly, there are public announcements about the National Tribal Development policy, but no consultations or initiatives have happened till now. The promise of granting Scheduled Tribe status to Adivasis of Assam working in tea gardens has only been election rhetoric till now.

Adivasi Experiences of NDA-II Government's Performance

1. Non-Implementation of FRA

In 2018, the Prime Minister himself made the ambitious announcement that all kinds of individual and collective claims under the FRA would be settled in two months. For example, newspaper reports indicate that in Jharkhand's Latehar district, only 20-25 per cent of claims have been actually settled till now. Adivasi communities are being systematically denied their traditional rights by using legal loopholes and in many cases in Odisha, Chhattisgarh and Jharkhand, the government is watering down provisions to divert forest land for mining purposes. For example, in Latehar, a fake Gram Sabha consent was submitted for getting permission for a coal mine. In another instance in Chhattisgarh, officials did not recognize FRA claims for 12 villages because an iron ore mine is proposed in that area. In Surguja district, the government actually cancelled a Community Forest Resource (CFR) because the Adani Group had plans to set up a mining project. In this way, thousands of CFRs have been denied in favour of promoting mining activity in the forested region.[1]

2. Non-Implementation of the TSP

The implementation of the TSP has been a farcical exercise since its inception in 1974. Under this policy, the Union and the state governments are required to have separate fund allocations in proportion to the Adivasi population in schemes which are directly beneficial to the community. But experience shows that not in a single year has the Union government followed this policy in letter and spirit.

If we analyse the trends of TSP allocations at the Union level for the past five years, there is a serious denial of financial resources due to the tribal communities of the country. Not in a single year has the allocation been more than 5.5 per cent, whereas the policy requires that allocations under TSP must be at least 7.5 per cent of the total development outlay. This is a gross denial of Adivasi development rights. There are significant budget cuts in the programmes meant for development of Primitive Tribal Groups, from scholarships, appointment of language teachers and Panchayat training programmes.

CAG Audit of the TSP: In 2014–15, the Comptroller and Auditor General (CAG) of India initiated a countrywide audit of TSP-sponsored programmes. The report, released in 2015, found that notional allocations on a large scale have been made by the government especially in education and health sector, which is totally unacceptable. There is evidence that although the Central ministry allocates TSP money in Centrally sponsored schemes, it doesn't go to states. Apart from this, there are major diversions of funds from the TSP by Central ministries and serious action needs to be taken. But the CAG report recommendations have been intentionally buried and the government is following the same trend all over again.

Scheduled Tribe Component (STC): Five-Year Trend Analysis of Union Budget FYs 2014–19 (Rs crore)

S.No.	Financial Year	Total Plan Outlay/ CS+CSS Schemes [A]	Due as per Special Component Plan Guideline (8.6 per cent to A) [B]	TSP/STC Allocation (Statement 10B of BE) [C]	Proportion of TSP/STC Allocation (C per cent to A) [D]	Gap in Allocation— ST [B]–[C] [E]	Total Targeted Schemes— ST [F]	Total Non-Targeted Schemes— ST [G]	Total Gap— ST [E+G] [H]
1	2014–15 (BE)	5,75,000	49,450	32,348	5.63 per cent	17,102	8,497	23,851	40,953
2	2015–16 (BE)	4,65,277	40,014	20,000	4.30 per cent	20,014	7,469	12,531	32,545
3	2016–17 (BE)	5,50,010	47,301	24,005	4.3 per cent	23,295	8,791	15,215	38,510
4	2017–18 (BE)	5,88,025	50,570	31,920	5.43 per cent	18,651	15,643	16,276	34,927
5	2018–19 (BE)	8,63,944	74,299	39,135	4.53 per cent	35,164	19,623	19,512	54,676
	Total	2,178,312	261,634	1,47,407	6.77 per cent	1,14,227	60,023	87,385	201,612

Note: Post-plan and non-plan merger in 2017–18, the due amount for the Scheduled Tribes component is calculated as 8.6 per cent of those Central sector schemes and Centrally sponsored schemes that have made allocations to the welfare of SCs as per statement 10B.

(Source: Budget Circular 2018–19 (OM) MoF No. (F).2(1)-B(CDN)/2017, dated 30 December 2016, Union Budget Expenditure Profile Vol. 1, 2014–15 to 2018–19)

3. Passing of the MMDR Amendment Act

Despite clear evidence of the adverse impact of mining on Adivasi communities in the form of massive displacement, land alienation and destruction of natural habitats, the NDA-II government managed to pass the MMDR Amendment Act without any sincere engagement with stakeholders. This amendment is crucial because it has undone the efforts of civil society in formulating the original Act which in principle had made way for benefit sharing and participation of communities in the mining process. For instance, as per the 2011 bill, notification of public lands for all types of mining concessions had to be done in consultation with the Gram Sabha or district council in Fifth and Sixth Schedule areas. In non-Schedule areas, district panchayats were required to be consulted, but this clause has been removed in the 2015 amendments. Similarly, the MMDR 2015 Act has denied and removed the provision of compensation, rehabilitation and resettlement of persons having usufruct and traditional rights over land and resources which were there in the 2011 Bill. Now all compensation, rehabilitation and resettlement are limited to occupational rights. The MMDR 2015 Act does not safeguard the rights of communities, discourages consultation and excludes affected people from decision-making on the mining sector.

4. Suppressing the Xaxa Committee HLC Report

In 2013, the UPA government formed a high-level committee (HLC) chaired by Prof. Virginius Xaxa to look into the socio-economic issues faced by the Adivasis and suggest a future action plan. The committee submitted its report[2] to the tribal ministry, presenting an in-depth analysis of how development activities and strategies in India have increased the socio-economic gulf between tribals and the rest of the citizens of India and left the former worse off on many counts. The report says that about

40 per cent of all people displaced in India due to development activity have been tribals. Adivasi communities face disregard for their values and culture, breach of protective legislations, serious material and social deprivation and aggressive resource alienation. The panel recommended radical changes to the laws, regulations and rules to protect Adivasi communities from land alienation and to ensure their rights over resources are handed back and protected. The report also laid out an overhauled, expansive and detailed framework for providing better education, health and opportunities to tribal communities across the country. If the recommendations of the Xaxa committee are implemented, it will surely have an empowering effect on Adivasi communities. But the present government has suppressed the HLC report and there has been no follow-up or discussion raised by the committee.

5. Violence against Adivasis in LWE Areas

State sponsored and extremist violence continues unabated on Adivasi communities, especially in central India. The perpetrators of violence enjoy total immunity while thousands of innocent Adivasis are tortured, jailed, killed or forced to migrate to safer places. Adivasi women are the worst sufferers and experience rape and sexual assault on a day-to-day basis. The government has pitted Adivasis against Adivasis by arming them with deadly weapons to assist armed forces in raiding and destroying Adivasi villages. There is a clear support for mining companies as it will help to clear the mineral rich region for mining activities.

6. Plight of the Tea Tribes

There are around seventy lakh Adivasis who had migrated from the Chotanagpur region during the pre-Independence period to work in the tea gardens of Assam. These migrant Adivasis face serious problems because many of the tea gardens have closed and there are several cases of starvation deaths. These tea tribes are not recognized as Scheduled Tribes, therefore they are unable to access entitlements or basic amenities. Although several political parties have promised to resolve their issues, this remains mostly electoral rhetoric. In the 2014 general elections, the Adivasis in tea gardens had supported the NDA on the promise that they would be provided ST status but the promises have not materialized yet.

7. Increasing Communalization of Adivasis

Sister organizations of the BJP, like the ABVKA and Saraswati Shishu Mandir, have been working in Adivasi areas for decades, preparing a strong cadre base by following the agenda of assimilation in the Hindu religion. With the present government, these organizations have also got administrative support and resources to implement their communal agenda in Adivasi areas. As a result, there have been several attacks on minority organizations, civil society groups, scholars and journalists who work among the Adivasis.[3] Last year, the ABVKA released a national vision document suggesting a comprehensive action plan for working in Adivasi areas. Apart from development issues, there was also a demand for a stringent anti-conversion law which has been used as a tool to divide the Adivasi communities on the lines of religion. The communal agenda of these organizations has gradually created a fear among people who don't subscribe to the dominant discourse of assimilating Adivasis into the Hindu fold. As a result, the harmonious relationship between various Adivasi and forest-dependent communities have been broken and communal violence is also increasingly experienced in Adivasi areas.

In order to work towards the real empowerment process of Adivasi communities, there is a need for all concerned individuals and organizations who are committed to peace, reconciliation and justice to come on a common platform to ensure cultural, economic and political rights of the most marginalized communities.

Editor's Note: This essay was written by Abhay Xaxa towards the last year of the NDA government in 2019, before the elections and the return of the NDA to power again. The instances provided by the author are based on newspaper reports of 2018. It is difficult to track down each and every media report to which Abhay Xaxa alludes in this essay.

The Life and Legacy of Abhay Xaxa[1]

Chitrangada Choudhury and Aniket Aga

On 18 March 2015, near the Barwadih block office in Jharkhand's Latehar district, a group of about sixty Adivasi men publicly defecated on copies of the Narendra Modi government's bill to amend the 2013 Right to Fair Compensation and Transparency in Land Acquisition, Rehabilitation and Resettlement Act. The bill sought to weaken the hard-won and long overdue safeguards of social impact assessment and informed consent to acquisition. It was a throwback to when state and industry could forcibly displace rural—especially Adivasi—communities and acquire their land and common property resources.

The protest at Barwadih, organized by the National Campaign on Adivasi Rights, got the mainstream media to briefly focus on Adivasi dispossession. The campaign's Abhay Flavian Xaxa, a young sociologist, Oraon Adivasi activist and writer, had also organized a march against the bill the previous day in his native village Jashpur, in Chhattisgarh, which unfolded under heavy police presence and scant media attention. In Barwadih, Xaxa countered the charge of 'uncivility':

If our poop protest is considered uncivil, then tell me what is civil in this country. Displacing millions of Adivasis for satisfying corporate greed is civil? Killing thousands of unarmed Adivasis

146

in [the] name of counter insurgency is civil? Trafficking lakhs of innocent . . . Adivasi girls to cities is civil? Blatantly cheating the Adivasis from the constitutional promises is civil? What type of civility do you expect from a person who was uprooted from their land not once, but twice in the name of national interest and is now threatened for a third time?[2]

Sharp, creative, and multi-faceted, Abhay Xaxa could articulate the hypocrisies of Indian society in salty metaphors. He deftly showed how policies drafted in high offices and in thrall to special economic interests affected India's marginalized in devastating ways. On 14 March 2020, while on a visit to Siliguri to meet with tribal groups, Abhay suffered a heart attack and passed away within minutes. He is survived by his partner Vani and children Sara and Manav. Abhay's shock death has left many of us reflecting on an activist-intellectual with a large heart and a sense of mischief, whom our society let die at the mere age of forty-three.

The loss was best articulated by the polymath and founder of the Adivasi Academy, Ganesh Devy, as he recalled his first meeting in 2006 with Abhay. 'Three decades ago, in a conversation at the Adivasi Academy, [historian] Ramachandra Guha had asked me, "Why is it that there has been no Ambedkar among Adivasis?" Nearly ten years later, as I was interviewing Abhay (for a fellowship), this question surfaced in my memory. I felt as if Abhay could probably be the answer for that question. In my subsequent conversations with him, and through his work in bringing young Adivasis together for re-thinking the entire Adivasi question in India, Abhay continued to keep that hope alive in my heart.'

The Making of an Indigenous Activist

Abhay defined himself thus: 'Sociologist by profession, Indigenous Activist by heart!' From his formative years in Chhattisgarh as a leader in Adivasi student unions and as a researcher-activist, to the past decade in Delhi, working with Dalit and Adivasi networks, alongside acquiring a PhD in Sociology at Jawaharlal Nehru University, Abhay's motivating force was justice. He cared for justice on all fronts: social, economic, environmental and in the realm of education and knowledge production.

Abhay's drive was born in a milieu of social discrimination, state violence and economic exploitation at the hands of the upper castes, moneylenders and contractors, which he witnessed through his childhood and as a college student. For example, when Abhay was in secondary school, he tasted arbitrary state power of a kind which regularly assaults the dignity of many Adivasis. A forest guard caught him collecting firewood near the village and arrested him under the colonial-era Indian Forest Act, 1927.

Abhay, who was collecting the firewood to prepare the day's meal at his school hostel, was eventually released on bail. In 2019, when the Supreme Court ordered the eviction of lakhs of Adivasis and forest dwellers from their land, Abhay drew on his own experiences to urgently mobilize civil society and grassroots groups and lobby with governments. He planned protests against the ruling, which he called the outcome of 'Brahmanical environmentalism'. The court eventually put the ruling on hold.

In the early 1990s, Abhay dropped out of college due to economic hardship in the family. His father, one of the first Adivasi judges in Madhya Pradesh, had lost his job—a termination Abhay ascribed to caste prejudice. Abhay briefly ran his own business by purchasing a jeep—through a government loan scheme for Scheduled Tribes—to ferry villagers around Jashpur. As he recalled with pride, the jeep at that time was the first in the district to be owned and run by an Adivasi and which was a success because it did not overcharge or cheat villagers.

Abhay eventually returned to college, convinced by the need to 'educate and agitate'. His younger brother Ajay told us that it was in these years that Abhay became active as an organizer and leader in the Adivasi Students Union, raising issues such as unpaid scholarships, kerosene for the students, high dropout rates, caste discrimination and poor conditions of Adivasi hostels.

As Abhay recounted in an interview in 2011 to a portal for Dalit and Adivasi students, his growing up years made him sad, bitter and angry, but also steeled him to challenge life-long social exclusion. He observed, 'To be able to continue studies and stay in Adivasi hostels, (the students) just needed to be given 100 kg of rice and 20 kg of pulses per year, but that too they could not afford. I feel extremely fortunate to be able to complete my studies, though with some breaks in between due to finances. I think this created a deep impact in my mind and I was always very conscious about this. And as I grew up, I started looking for the answers.'

After graduating in sociology and law, Abhay briefly worked in Hindi news media, but found editors hostile to his concerns. He took up research and activism, working across social movements, research institutions and NGOs on development-induced displacement, distress migration, bonded labour and fair wages for forest workers such as tendu leaf pickers.

In 2007, he became the first Adivasi student from Chhattisgarh to win the Ford Foundation International Fellowship for postgraduate study at the University of Sussex. This was the fellowship for which Devy had interviewed Abhay. Abhay chose to study anthropology. As he laughingly explained in the 2011 interview: 'I wanted to see what non-Adivasis have written about us.'

The Years of Struggle

Despite his struggles or perhaps because of them, Abhay was never bitter or invested in drawing hard boundaries of insider/outsider. As Devy pointed out, 'Abhay was a thinker among the Adivasis, and an Adivasi among thinkers. He could be equally restless in both worlds. He was genuinely interested in ideas and had an intellectual bandwidth that reminded me of another friend I lost too early, D.R. Nagaraj, the thinker and writer from Karnataka.'

The year at Sussex broadened Abhay's world and put him in touch with international discourses on indigenous peoples and movements, recalled Azizur Rahman, a close friend from the fellowship cohort and now an Asian Development Bank consultant. Xavier Dias, a veteran activist in Jharkhand, concurred: 'Abhay returned with a fire in his heart, restless to fight for his people, and to give them the best options.'

These were the years when Adivasi communities of central-eastern India's forested mineral belt were facing the brunt of resource grabs on a massive scale, due to mining and land acquisition projects. Also, the state-Maoist conflict was escalating across the region, bringing counter-insurgency operations, militarization, vigilante violence and human rights abuses. Abhay plunged into the task of highlighting these excesses. It was at one such programme held in Ranchi in 2010 on extrajudicial 'encounter' killings that we first met Abhay. We were struck by how thoughtful and articulate he was, even as he wore his challenges lightly with an infectious smile.

Courage was a liability when the state was tarring activism and dissent as 'Maoist activity'. Frontline Adivasi activists like Abhay were particularly vulnerable.

Stan Swamy, a Jesuit anthropologist in Ranchi recalled, 'The Abhay I knew was literally a (without) bhay (fear). He would barge into a government office and blast the officer for what he was doing against Adivasis or for what he was not doing that he should have done for the Adivasi.' Frontline Adivasi activists like Abhay, Bastar's Soni Sori and Jharkhand's Gladson Dungdung, were particularly vulnerable to harassment and criminalization. As Swamy recalls, 'Within a short time it was communicated to Abhay that if he went on doing what he was, he would find himself in jail indefinitely with multiple cases against him.'

Based in Delhi, Abhay initially worked as a Research Fellow at the Indian Institute of Dalit Studies and from 2012–19 as a programme coordinator with the National Campaign on Dalit Human Rights (NCDHR). He had come to believe in the importance of cross-learning between Dalit and Adivasi movements across issues such as discrimination in public spending and higher education, the poor enforcement of the Prevention of Atrocities Act and forest and land rights programmes. Close friend and NCDHR colleague

Beena Pallical recounted, 'He constantly argued for the need for Dalit and Adivasi struggles to move together, given our common experiences of exclusion and exploitation.'

Travelling extensively, Abhay also became an anchor for grassroots groups, activists, student bodies and scholars across the country, serving as convener for the National Campaign for Adivasi Rights and a co-convener of the Tribal Intellectual Collective. Koraput-based researcher Sharanya Nayak recalled Abhay's visit to Malkangiri to look at the issue of bonded labour and their deep friendship since: 'He was very perceptive and could make deep connections between people's experiences and the larger systemic violence that is happening to the indigenous peoples.'

Over the years, Dias said, 'Abhay developed his own understanding of the law, budgets, tribal sub-plans and policies in scheduled areas, and made training modules, thinking about what would empower his people.' He developed a special interest in analysing illegal diversions and shortfalls in budgetary allocations for Scheduled Tribes, which effectively had robbed Adivasis over decades of their statutory due. 'On budget day, Abhay would be that rare voice on TV who would be telling us what it meant for tribal communities,' said Abhay's doctoral thesis supervisor L. Lam Khan Piang. 'There is nobody to do that now.'

Building Knowledge for Social Change

Abhay's doctoral work at Jawaharlal Nehru University (JNU) melded his interests in sociology and law. He researched how Jharkhand's land laws marginalized Adivasi communities and how Adivasi responses shaped their relationship with the Indian state. The questions that Abhay—and many other scholars like him—posed came from his immediate lives and struggles, but they often find a hostile and alienating environment within the rigid conventions of the academy. Abhay had to change supervisors mid research and when he submitted his thesis in 2018, he called it the 'most arduous journey of his life'.

As his supervisor Piang remarked, Abhay was consumed with taking his knowledge to marginalized spaces and with social change. 'He was full of ideas and rarely on campus. I would ask, "Where are you Abhay?" and he would be travelling across the country, holding training workshops or presenting papers.'

Over his last year, Abhay had begun experimenting with interactive formats on social media to communicate challenges like the 2019 Supreme Court eviction order more widely. In March 2019, Abhay came together with the digital platform Adivasi Lives Matter and us to film a primer[3] for Adivasi and forest-dwelling communities. It explained their rights to free, prior, informed consent under the Forest Rights Act in the face of forest land grabs by the powerful state-corporate combine.

Abhay's more recent writings pushed the frontiers of imagination on Adivasiyat: on how to rescue indigenity from identitarianism and link it to democracy, environmental justice, climate change and sustainability. Over the past year, he was editing a volume on Adivasi communities in a multi-part series for Penguin Random House India, titled Rethinking India. Friends like Nayak and Ankush Vengurlekar, the founder of Adivasi Lives Matter, asserted that Abhay's aim was to rally more and more people in the cause of Adivasiyat. As his NCDHR colleagues Pallical and N. Paul Divakar wrote in a recent obituary, 'He refused to accept Adivasis as an esoteric-ethnic community, but also felt that they bring a strength of sustainability, which the wider society needs to accept.'[4]

In a talk Abhay delivered at Ashoka University in February 2019, he elaborated on the concept of 'indigenocracy': bringing together notions of citizenship with responsibility towards one another and the environment. He also raised troubling questions about why the fields of environmental studies, climate change and sustainability persisted in excluding Adivasis and forest-dwelling communities. Why were universities, Forest Departments or environmental NGOs, he asked, hostile to staffing Adivasi scholars and leaders, and recognizing the knowledge and contributions of these communities in nurturing forest ecosystems?

As Abhay often pointed in public meetings on higher education, our universities had failed students from marginalized backgrounds, like Rohith Vemula and Payal Tadvi. Equally, they have failed to make room for teachers like Abhay. Just 2.2 per cent of the teaching staff in higher education come from Scheduled Tribe backgrounds, as per a 2017–18 survey.[5] Behind these statistics lie the perseverance, struggles and defeats of numerous scholars like Abhay.

On getting his doctorate, Abhay was keen to relocate to central-east India so that he could work closely with students from marginalized communities and be closer to frontline challenges and his family in Jashpur. But he found himself up against damaging red tape, like when universities did not recognize his Sussex master's degree since it had a duration of a year as opposed to the two-year programme in India. He felt particularly crushed when St Xavier's College in Ranchi did not select him for a teaching position.

In conversations with us over the past year, Abhay often expressed a sense of fatigue and dejection. Seeing the brutal crackdown on civil society organizations and cases filed against activists and scholars like Sudha Bharadwaj, Stan Swamy and Anand Teltumbde, Abhay had mused to us, 'I am not sure if tomorrow, the government were to do away with reservations for Dalits and Adivasis, people will be able to come together and protest in India.' He also suffered bouts of poor health. As he told an interviewer in 2019, 'This is a long fight.'[6] His poem 'A Republic of Lost Memory' reflected his anguish:

Dear Republic,
When your best citizens are killed on the streets,
and piled in the jails.
While the traitors adorn your high offices.
Something is terribly wrong with you!

No Academic Attended

There has been a silence from social scientists and the wider academia, about the snuffing out of one of its brightest stars. It is largely students' groups, Dalit and Adivasi networks and alternative media outlets who have marked Abhay's death: another parallel with Rohith Vemula and Payal Tadvi.

In a recent paper Abhay had shared with us, he reflected on the 'epistemic violence' in online spaces that deny marginalized peoples the capacity to learn and know. Privileged Indians see Adivasis, Dalits and Bahujans through casteist prejudice and caricatures and encounter them largely as cheap labour. As powerful essays in *The India Forum* by the historian Maroona Murmu and the economist Aditi Priya testify, even the academic establishment remains hostile to their struggles.[7] It does not celebrate their success and creativity in life and remains largely indifferent to their deaths.

A day after Abhay was brought back from Siliguri to be buried in Jashpur, his close friend and writer Gladson Dungdung piercingly wrote: 'If someone this qualified is humiliated in this way, will his mind be at peace? Will he not suffer a heart attack? But we will keep fighting, for recognition, for our identity, for our earth, for our forests, hills and rivers.'

'It takes a long time to incubate an organic intellectual, and leader like Abhay,' Dias reflected with sadness. 'In these past years, I felt that he was coming into his own. He was becoming someone who could have mobilized Adivasi people, without getting absorbed into the electoral party system and being co-opted into doing its bidding. Which is why his death at this young age is so troubling.'

In early March, just days before his sudden death, Abhay had spoken on the phone with his younger brother Ajay. In the conversation, Abhay had returned to a recurrent concern: 'Dada talked about our village and said we must do something to ensure economic opportunities here itself, so that our people do not have to migrate to the cities and be exploited.' As Ajay spoke to us, the media was awash with images of thousands of desperate migrants abandoned by the government and the cities, trying to flee home to their villages in the face of a criminally ill-planned lockdown. The absence of Abhay's voice, calling for a more just and humane India, rang loud.

Notes

Safeguarding and Deepening the Promise of India for Adivasis

1   Christophe Jaffrelot and A. Kalaiyarasan, 'Margins of New India', *Indian Express*, 2018, https://indianexpress.com/article/opinion/columns/mp-chhattisgarh-election-tribal-development-raman-singh-shivraj-chouhan-5465964/

2   N.C. Saxena, *What Ails the IAS and Why It Fails to Deliver: An Insider's View* (Sage Publications India, 2019)

3   'District Fact Sheet, Koraput, Odisha', *National Family Health Survey-4*, 2015-16, http://rchiips.org/nfhs/FCTS/OR/OR_FactSheet_398_Koraput.pdf

4   Planning Commission, *MTA 2000, Mid-term appraisal of the 9th Plan* (New Delhi).

5   'Tribal: Victims of Development Projects – India's Forced Displacement Policy and Practice', 2012, https://socialissuesindia.files.wordpress.com/2012/09/tribal-displacement-in-india.pdf

6   'Niyamgiri Triumph' *Economic and Political Weekly*, vol. 45, no. 35, 2010, p. 7., www.jstor.org/stable/25742009

7   'In the Supreme Court of India, Civil Original Jurisdiction', Writ Petition (Civil) No. 180 of 2011, Orissa Mining Corporation (Petitioner) versus Ministry of Environment & Forests & Others (Respondents). K.S. Radhakrishnan was the judge, p. 22.

8   'Niyamgiri Triumph', 2010, op. cited, p. 7.

9 N.C. Saxena, *Livelihood Diversification and Non-Timber Forest Products in Orissa: Wider Lessons on the Scope for Policy Change?* (London, Overseas Development Institute, 2003).
10 Ibid.
11 Government of India, Ministry of Tribal Affairs, *Status report on the implementation of the Scheduled Tribes and Other Traditional Forest Dwellers (Recognition of Forest Rights) Act, 2006.*
12 Ibid.

Tribal Development in Fifth Schedule Areas: Affirmative Action or Unequal Exchange?

1 K.S. Singh (2002), *Birsa Munda and His Movement 1872-1901: A Study of a Millenarian Movement in Chotanagpur* (Kolkata, Seagull Books, 2002); S. Bosu Mullick, *Jharkhand Movement: A Historical Analysis*, Mrinal Miri (ed.), *Continuity and Change in Tribal Society* (Shimla, IIAS, 1993), pp. 437–462.
2 V.R. Raghavaiah, *Tribal Revolts in Chronological Order: 1778-1971*, A.R. Desai (ed.), *Peasant Struggles in India* (Bombay, OUP, 1979); S. Bosu Mullick, *Jharkhand Movement: A Historical Analysis*, Mrinal Miri (ed.), *Continuity and Change in Tribal Society* (Shimla, IIAS, 1993), pp. 437–462.
3 B.P. Misra, Keynote Address at National Seminar on Governance, Socio-Economic Disparity and Unrest in 'Scheduled Areas' of India, (Tata Institute of Social Sciences, Guwahati Campus, 22-24 November 2012).
4 T.H. Marshall, *Class, Citizenship and Social Development* (Chicago, Chicago University Press, 1977).
5 T.H. Marshall, *Class, Citizenship and Social Development* (Chicago, Chicago University Press, 1977), pp 78–91.
6 Myron Weiner, *Summary Comments on the Affirmative Action Workshop* (Development and Democracy, September: 81–86, 1993).
7 Planning Commission, Govt of India, *Report of the Steering Committee on Empowering the Scheduled Tribes for the Tenth Five Year Plan (2002–2007)*, (New Delhi, Planning Commission, 2001).

8   Bharat Chandra Rout, *Affirmative Action for Weaker Sections of Society in Institutions of Higher Education in India* (PhD thesis, National University of Educational Planning and Administration, 2014).

9   Planning Commission, Govt of India, *Tenth Five Year Plan 2002–07* (New Delhi, Planning Commission, 2003–04), pp. 134.

10 Ibid., p. 135.

11 Planning Commission, Govt of India, *Report of the Steering Committee on Empowering the Scheduled Tribes for the Tenth Five Year Plan (2002–2007)*, (New Delhi, Planning Commission, 2001); Devath Suresh, *Tribal Development Through Five Year Plans in India- An Overview* [The Dawn Journal, 3(1), 2014], pp. 794-816.

12 Ibid.

13 Planning Commission, Govt of India, *Report of the Steering Committee on Empowering the Scheduled Tribes for the Tenth Five Year Plan (2002–2007)*, (New Delhi, Planning Commission, 2001).

14 Ministry of Tribal Affairs, Government of India and UNDP, *Land and Governance under the Fifth Schedule: An Overview of the Law* (Undated)

15 Government of India (Planning Commission). 2001. Report of the Steering Committee on Empowering the Scheduled Tribes for the Tenth Five Year Plan (2002–2007), (New Delhi, Planning Commission).

16 Ibid.

17 Ministry of Tribal Affairs, Govt. of India, 2014. *Report of the High Level Committee on Socio-economic and Health Status of Tribal Communities in India.*

18 Subhash C. Kashyap, *National Policy Studies* [New Delhi, Tata McGraw-Hill Publishing Company Ltd., (Published for the Lok Sabha Secretariat), 1990].

19 Ibid., p. 316.

20 Madhu Sarin, 2005 *Scheduled Tribes Bill 2005: A Comment* in *Economic and Political Weekly*, XL (21), pp. 2131-2134.

21 Ibid.

22 S.C. Patnaik, *Dependent Economy of North East Region of India and Alternative Planning Techniques* (Paper presented at the National Seminar on Institutional Economics, North-Eastern Hill University, Shillong, 1987).

23 Nirmal Sengupta, 1979. *Class structure in Jharkhand*, National Labour Institute Bulletin, 5 (7–8).

24 Xaxa, Virginius, *Tribes and Social Exclusion, Occasional Paper No. 2, CSSC–UNICEF* (Kolkata, Social Inclusion Cell, 2011).

25 M. Areeparampil, *Industries, Mines and Dispossession of Indigenous Peoples: The Case of Chotanagpur*, W. Fernandes and E. Ganguly Thukral (eds), *Development, Displacement and Rehabilitation* (New Delhi, Indian Social Institute, 1989).

26 S.M. Patnaik, *Displacement, Rehabilitation and Social Change* (New Delhi, Inter-India Publications, 1996).

27 Ibid.

28 Ashok Mathur, *An Overview of the Jharkhand Economy and Perspectives for Human Development* (Ranchi, Background paper read at the National Seminar on Growth and Human Development in Jharkhand: Perspectives and Policies, 4–5 July 2008).

References

M. Areeparampil, *Industries, Mines and Dispossession of Indigenous Peoples: The Case of Chotanagpur*, W. Fernandes and E. Ganguly Thukral (eds), *Development, Displacement and Rehabilitation* (New Delhi, Indian Social Institute, 1989)

S. Bosu Mullick, *Jharkhand Movement: A Historical Analysis*, Mrinal Miri (ed.), *Continuity and Change in Tribal Society* (Shimla, IIAS, 1993), pp. 437-462.

Ministry of Tribal Affairs, Government of India and UNDP, *Land and Governance under the Fifth Schedule: An Overview of the Law* (Undated).

Planning Commission, Govt of India, *Report of the Steering Committee on Empowering the Scheduled Tribes for the Tenth Five Year Plan (2002-2007)*, (New Delhi, Planning Commission, 2001).

Planning Commission, Govt of India, *Tenth Five Year Plan 2002-07* (New Delhi, Planning Commission, 2003-04), chapter 4.2, pp. 443-474.

Ministry of Tribal Affairs, Govt of India, *Report of the Working Group on Empowerment of Scheduled Tribes for the Eleventh Five Year Plan (2007–2012)*, (New Delhi, Ministry of Tribal Affairs, 2007).

Ministry of Tribal Affairs, Govt of India, *Report of the High Level Committee on Socio-economic and Heath Status of Tribal Communities in India* (New Delhi, Ministry of Tribal Affairs, 2014).

Subhash C. Kashyap, *National Policy Studies* [New Delhi, Tata McGraw-Hill Publishing Company Ltd (Published for the Lok Sabha Secretariat), 1990].

T.H. Marshall, *Class, Citizenship and Social Development* (Chicago, Chicago University Press, 1977).

Ashok Mathur, *An Overview of the Jharkhand Economy and Perspectives for Human Development* (Ranchi, Background paper read at the National Seminar on Growth and Human Development in Jharkhand: Perspectives and Policies, 4–5 July 2008).

B.P. Misra, Keynote Address at National Seminar on Governance, Socio-Economic Disparity and Unrest in 'Scheduled Areas' of India, Tata Institute of Social Sciences, Guwahati Campus, 22-24 November 2012).

S.C. Patnaik, *Dependent Economy of North East Region of India and Alternative Planning Techniques* (Paper presented at the National Seminar on Institutional Economics, North-Eastern Hill University, Shillong, 1987).

S.M. Patnaik, *Displacement, Rehabilitation and Social Change* (New Delhi, Inter-India Publications, 1996).

V.R. Raghavaiah, *Tribal Revolts in Chronological Order: 1778-1971*, A.R. Desai (ed.), *Peasant Struggles in India* (Bombay, OUP, 1979).

Bharat Chandra Rout, *Affirmative Action for Weaker Sections of Society in Institutions of Higher Education in India* (PhD thesis, National University of Educational Planning and Administration, 2014).

Madhu Sarin, 2005 *Scheduled Tribes Bill 2005: A Comment* in *Economic and Political Weekly*, XL (21), pp. 2131-2134.

Nirmal Sengupta, 1979. *Class structure in Jharkhand*, National Labour Institute Bulletin, 5 (7-8).

K.S. Singh, *Birsa Munda and His Movement 1872-1901: A Study of a Millenarian Movement in Chotanagpur* (Kolkata, Seagull Books, 2002).

Devath Suresh, *Tribal Development Through Five Year Plans in India- An Overview* [The Dawn Journal, 3(1), 2014], pp. 794-816.

Sukhadeo Thorat, *Tribal Deprivation and Poverty in India: A Macro-Analysis*, Joseph Bara (ed.), *Ordeals and Voices of the Indigenous Tribal People of India* (Guwahati, Indian Confederation of Indigenous and Tribal Peoples, North-East Zone, 2006), pp. 180-202.

Myron Weiner, *Summary Comments on the Affirmative Action Workshop* (Development and Democracy, September: 81-86, 1993).

Virginius Xaxa, *Tribes and Social Exclusion, Occasional Paper No.2, CSSC-UNICEF* (Kolkata, Social Inclusion Cell, 2011).

Tribal Heritage and People's Rights

1   David Reich, 2018.
2   Census of India, 2011.
3   'Transforming Institutions and Question of Forest Conservation: A Historical Documentation of Forest Policies in India', C.P.R. Environmental Education Centre, http://cpreec.org
4   Verrier Elwin, *A Philosophy for NEFA* (Oxford, 1959, Second Revised Edition, 2008).
5   Constituent Assembly debates, *Constituent Assembly of India: Volume VII, Part IX* (4 November 1948).
6   Constituent Assembly debates, *Constituent Assembly of India: Volume VII, Part IX* (4 November 1948).
7   Jawaharlal Nehru's endorsement of Verrier Elwin's concept of Panchsheel, in relation to Tribals in India, in his foreword to *A Philosophy for NEFA* (Oxford, 1959, Second Revised Edition, 2008)
8   Ibid.
9   D. Isaac Devadoss, 'Christian Identity, Hindu Nationalism and Religious Communal Violence in India with Special Reference to Kandhamal, Odisha', 2018, https://ukzn-dspace.ukzn.ac.za/bitstream/handle/10413/17015/Devadoss_Devairakkam_Isaac_2019.pdf
10 C.R. Bijoy, 'Policy brief on Panchayat Raj (Extension to Scheduled Areas) Act of 1996', *UNDP*, 2012, http://undp.org/content/dam/india/docs/UNDP-Policy-Brief-on-PESA.pdf
11 Census of India, 2011 data.
12 'State / UT wise overall population, ST population, percentage of STs in India / State to total population of India / State and percentage of STs in the State to total ST population', *Ministry of Tribal Affairs, Government of India*, https://tribal.nic.in/downloads/statistics/Statistics8518.pdf
13 Census 2011 data.

14 *Displacement and Rehabilitation of People Due to Developmental Projects*,
Library and Reference, Research, Documentation and Information
Service (LARRDIS) members' reference service reference note.
No.30/RN/Ref./December/2013, Lok Sabha Secretariat,
Parliament.

15 Abhijit Mohanty, 'Armed With a Toothless Law, the Plight of the
Adivasi Worsens', The Wire, 2017, https://thewire.in/politics/pesa-
tribal-adivasi-rights

16 'Supreme Court Cases', *Supreme Court Cases Weekly*, https://www.
scconline.com/blog/post/tag/supreme-court-cases/

17 C.R. Bijoy, 'Why Is the Government Afraid of Implementing the
Forest Rights Act?', The Wire, 2020, https://science.thewire.in/
environment/community-forest-resources-forest-rights-act-2006-
ministry-of-tribal-affairs-implementation-gram-sabha/

18 Dr Sukhadeo Thorat, 'Exclusionary practices are deeply pervasive',
Frontline, 2016, https://frontline.thehindu.com/cover-story/
exclusionary-practices-are-deeply-pervasive/article8183610.ece.
A report prepared by Sukhadeo Thorat, in his capacity as chairman
of the UGC, which offered statistics and its analysis focusing
on exclusion from education, it is clearly established that tribals
are among the worst sufferers when it comes to exclusion from
education in India.

The Question of Integration

1 Government of India, 'Scheduled castes and scheduled tribes, Census
2011', Ministry of Home Affairs, https://censusindia.gov.in/Census_
And_You/scheduled_castes_and_sceduled_tribes.aspx

2 The Permanent Settlement was an agreement between the East India
Company and Bengali landlords to fix revenues to be raised from
land. It was concluded in 1793 by the Company administration. It
formed one part of a larger body of legislation enacted, known as the
Cornwallis Code.

3 The Ryotwari system was a land revenue system in British India. It
allowed the government to deal directly with the cultivator ('ryot')
for revenue collection and gave the peasant freedom to give up or

acquire new land for cultivation. The peasant was assessed for only the lands he was cultivating.

4   The Indian Forest Act, 1927 was largely based on previous Indian Forest Acts implemented under the British. The most famous one was the Indian Forest Act of 1878. Both the 1878 and the 1927 acts sought to consolidate and reserve the areas having forest cover or significant wildlife, to regulate movement and transit of forest produce and duty leviable on timber and other forest produce. It also defines the procedure to be followed for declaring an area to be a Reserved Forest, a Protected Forest or a Village Forest.

5   Alpa Shah, *In the Shadow of the State: Indigenous Politics, Environmentalism and Insurgency in Jharkhand India* (Durham NC, Duke University Press, 2010).

6   Constituent Assembly debates, 19 December 1946 and 24 August 1949.

7   Rochana Bajpai, 'Constituent Assembly Debates and Minority Rights', *Economic and Political Weekly*, vol. 35, No. 21/22, 2000, pp. 1837-1845.

8   Prathama Banerjee, 'Writing the Adivasi: Some Historiographical Notes', *The Indian Economic and Social History Review*, vol. No. 53 (1), 2016, pp. 131-153.

9   B.R. Ambedkar, *Communal Deadlock and a Way to Solve It*, Vasant Moon (ed.), *Dr Babasaheb Ambedkar Writings and Speeches*, vol. 1, Bombay, (1945) 1989, pp. 355–79.

10   Ramachandra Guha, 'Adivasis, Naxalites and Indian Democracy', *Economic and Political Weekly*, vol. 42, No. 32, 11-17 August 2007, pp. 3305-3312.

11   Walter Fernandes, *Development Induced Displacement and Tribal Women*, Govind Chandra Rath (ed.), *Tribal Development in India: The Contemporary Debate* (Sage Publications, 2006).

12   Ibid.

13   Report of the Scheduled Areas and Scheduled Tribes Committee, Government Press, New Delhi, 1961.

14   28th and 29th reports of the Commissioner for Scheduled Castes and Scheduled Tribes, Government of India Press, New Delhi, 1988 and 1990.

15 Amartya Sen and Martha Nussbaum, *The Quality of Life* (Oxford University Press, 1993), p. 30.

16 Government of India, 'Scheduled castes and scheduled tribes, Census 2011', Ministry of Home Affairs, https://censusindia.gov.in/Census_And_You/scheduled_castes_and_sceduled_tribes.aspx

17 Panchayats (Extension To The Scheduled Areas) Act, 1996, No.40 OF 1996, https://tribal.nic.in/actRules/PESA.pdf.

18 Forest Rights Act, 2006; https://tribal.nic.in/FRA/data/FRARulesBook.pdf.

19 Pushparaj Deshpande, 'This is why the Congress is against BJP's afforestation efforts', *The Indian Express*, 29 June 2016, https://indianexpress.com/article/blogs/this-is-why-the-congress-is-against-bjps-afforestation-efforts/

20 The Right To Fair Compensation And Transparency In Land Acquisition, Rehabilitation And Resettlement Act, 2013, http://legislative.gov.in/sites/default/files/A2013-30.pdf.

21 Promises and Reality: Citizens' Report on four years of the NDA government 2014-18, Coordinated by Wada Na Todo Abhiyan, May 2018.

22 Vanvasi Kalyan Ashram is a constituent of the Sangh Parivar, the family of organizations affiliated with the Rashtriya Swayamsevak Sangh (RSS). It focuses on the welfare activities of Scheduled Tribes in remote areas of India and has branches throughout the country.

23 Mines and Minerals (Development and Regulation) Act 1957, https://mines.gov.in/writereaddata/UploadFile/MMDR%20Act,1957.pdf.

24 Ministry Of Environment, Forest and Climate Change, Government Of India, Rajya Sabha Unstarred Question No. 727 To Be Answered On 17 December 2018, https://164.100.158.235/question/annex/247/Au727.pdf.

25 https://www.mines.gov.in/writereaddata/UploadFile/The_Mines-and-Minerals_Amendment_Act,2015.pdf (last accessed on 12 October 2021).

26 Arvind Khare, 'Let's not miss the wood', *The Hindu,* 27 June 2015, https://www.thehindu.com/opinion/op-ed/lets-not-miss-the-wood/article7358626.ece.

27 Annual Report 2018-19, Ministry of Tribal Affairs, Government of India, https://tribal.nic.in/writereaddata/AnnualReport/AREnglish1819.pdf.

28 Ibid.

29 Ishaan Kukreti and Priya Ranjan Sahu, 'Forest Rights Act: Are state govts the real land mafias?', Down to Earth, 20 March 2019, https://www.downtoearth.org.in/news/forests/forest-rights-act-are-state-govts-the-real-land-mafias--63664.

30 National Tribal Advisory Council was set up in 2015 under the chairmanship of the Prime Minister for real-time monitoring of various tribal development programmes and schemes in the country.

31 Amendment To Indian Forest Act, 1927, https://forest.mizoram.gov.in/uploads/attachments/4bdb5e07743b1d97755783ec4d88459b/pages-226-proposed-amendments-to-ifa-dated-7032019.pdf.

32 Chitrangada Choudhury, 'All Political Parties Have Treated Adivasis as Disposable People', IndiaSpend, 28 April 2019, https://www.indiaspend.com/all-political-parties-have-treated-adivasis-as-disposable-people/ and https://www.indiatoday.in/news-analysis/story/draft-indian-forest-amendment-bill-2019-arming-state-to-undermine-rights-and-wellbeing-of-tribals-1578054-2019-08-07 (last accessed on 12 October 2021).

33 https://thewire.in/environment/government-withdraws-controversial-amendments-to-forest-rights-act (last accessed on 12 October 2021).

34 The National Tiger Conservation Authority (NTCA) was established in December 2005 following a recommendation of the Tiger Task Force, constituted by the Prime Minister of India for reorganized management of Project Tiger and the tiger reserves in India.

35 SC Record of Proceedings Writ Petition(S)(Civil) No(S). 109/2008 WILDLIFE FIRST & ORS. Petitioner(S) VERSUS Ministry of Environment & Forest & ORS. Respondent(S), http://www.indiaenvironmentportal.org.in/files/file/Forest-Rights-claims-SC-Order_13-Feb-2019.pdf.

36 The Compensatory Afforestation Fund Act, 2016, http://www.ukcampa.org.in/Docs/CAMPA%20Act%202016.pdf.

37 K. Raju and Pushparaj Deshpande, 'Posture and policy', *Indian Express*, 4 July 2017, https://indianexpress.com/article/opinion/columns/sc-sts-government-expenditure-posture-and-policy-4734001/.

38 Budget Circular 2018-19 (OM) MoF No. (F).2(1)-B(CDN)/2017, 30 December 2016, Union Budget Expenditure Profile, vol. 1, 2014-15 to 2018-19.

39 University Grants Commission Circular, No. F.1-5/2006 (SCT), 5 March 2018, https://www.ugc.ac.in/pdfnews/1121433_reservation_policy1-2018.pdf.

40 Akash Bisht, Why is Modi govt. blocking scholarships meant for SC/ST students, Catch News, 24 October 2017, http://www.catchnews.com/politics-news/why-is-modi-govt-blocking-scholarships-meant-for-sc-st-students-86750.html.

41 Calculated from MGNREGS portal, Ministry of Rural Development, Government of India and Census of India.

42 Ibid.

43 Nitin Sethi, 'Govt uses off-record WhatsApp, instructing states to cut back work for MNREGA', *Business Standard*, 29 October 2016, https://www.business-standard.com/article/economy-policy/govt-uses-off-record-whatsapp-instructing-states-to-cut-back-work-for-mnrega-116102400673_1.html.

44 Calculated from MGNREGS portal, Ministry of Rural Development, Government of India and Census of India.

45 'Vanvasi Kalyan Ashram — How RSS, a Congress stalwart & a Gandhian crystallised the idea', Arun Anand, The Print, 26 December 2020 (https://theprint.in/india/vanvasi-kalyan-ashram-how-rss-a-congress-stalwart-a-gandhian-crystallised-the-idea/574407/; last accessed on 23 July 2021).

46 'Adivasi vs Vanvasi: The Hinduization of Tribals in India', IDRF and the American Funding of Hindutva, 2002, Sabrang Communications & Publishing Pvt. Ltd, Mumbai, India (https://www.outlookindia.com/website/story/adivasi-vs-vanvasi-thehinduization-of-tribals-in-india/217974#endnote133 (last accessed 23 July 2021).

47 Ibid and https://samvada.org/files/Widening-Horizons.pdf.

48 Ibid.

49 https://niti.gov.in/planningcommission.gov.in/docs/reports/sereport/ser/ser_atro2410 (last accessed on 12 October 2021).

50 https://pib.gov.in/PressReleaseIframePage.aspx?PRID=1707576 (last accessed on 12 October 2021).

51 *Mahatma Gandhi: The Last Phase*, vol. II (1958), p. 65

52 Report of the High Level Committee chaired by Virginius Xaxa, Ministry of Tribal Affairs, Govt of India, 2014

53 National Policy on Tribals, http://www.mcrhrdi.gov.in/87fc/policies/NATIONAL%20POLICY%20ON%20TRIBALS.pdf.

Class Struggle and the Future of Adivasi Politics

1 Purushottam Thakur and Kamlesh Painkra, 'Jamlo's Last Journey Along a Locked Down Road', People's Archive of Rural India, 14 May 2020, https://ruralindiaonline.org/articles/jamlos-last-journey-along-a-locked-down-road/

2 The term semi-proletarian was first used by Lenin to refer to those people who depended both on wage labour and access to land for their livelihoods. Small and marginal peasants who are forced to do seasonal work for others may also be included within this category. These can be differentiated from the industrial and rural proletariat who depend fully on wage labour for their survival.

3 Jan Breman, *Footloose Labour: Working in India's Informal Economy* (Cambridge, Cambridge University Press, 1997).

4 Jens Lerche, *From 'rural labour' to 'classes of labour': class fragmentation, caste and class struggle at the bottom of the Indian labour hierarchy* in Barbara Harriss-White and Judith Heyer (eds), *Comparative Political Economy of Development: Africa and South Asia* (London, Routledge, 2010).

5 Vikas Rawal, *Changes in the Distribution of Operational Landholdings in Rural India: A Study of National Sample Survey Data* in *Review of Agrarian Studies*, vol. 32 (2).

6 National Sample Survey Organisation (NSSO), *Household Ownership and Operational Holdings in India (Jan to June 2013)* (Delhi, NSSO, 2015), pp. 14–18.

7 For the Nehruvian Panchsheel which structured the paradigm of tribal development, see Jawaharlal Nehru, *Approach to Tribes* in *Jawaharlal*

Nehru's Speeches, 1953-1957 (New Delhi, Nehru Memorial Fund), pp. 458–61.

8   Archana Prasad, *Against Ecological Romanticism: Verrier Elwin and the Making of an Anti-Modern Tribal Identity*, [Delhi, Three Essays (Second Edition), 2011].

9   Archana Prasad, *Neoliberalism, Tribal Survival and Agrarian Distress* in Alternate Budget Survey Group (eds), *Two Decades of Neoliberalism* (Danish Books, 2010).

10 Vijoo Krishnan, 'Against the Violence of Development', *Frontline*, 15 September 2017. For environmental law relaxation, see Archana Prasad, 'EIA Notification: Not Now, Not Ever', Newsclick, 8 May 2020, https://www.newsclick.in/EIA-Notification-2020-Lockdown-India-BJP-Government.

11 Archana Prasad, *Environmentalism and the Left: Contemporary Debates and Future Agendas in Tribal Areas* (Leftword, 2004).

12 Enacted as a part of the Constitution, the Fifth and Sixth Schedules provided some protection to tribal institutions. They also protected them from land alienation and oppression by non-local people. The degree of protection was far greater in the Sixth Schedule (applicable to the autonomous council areas of the North-east), than the Fifth Schedule which was applicable to central and eastern India. But the struggle for control over local resources gained momentum with the enactment of the Panchayat (Extension to Scheduled Areas) Act in 1994.

13 The material for this paragraph has been taken from a fact-finding report 'Brutal state repression against the non-violent Pathalgadi Movement: Report of fact finding inquiry in Pathalgadi villages of Jharkhand', https://counterviewfiles.files.wordpress.com/2019/11/report-of-pathalgadi-factfinding-inquiry-english.pdf, accessed on 10 June 2020.

14 Mendha Lekha in Gadchiroli, Maharashtra was one of the first villages to declare 'Gram Swaraj' or self-rule through the use of these laws in the early twenty-first century. They also invoked the Scheduled Tribes and Other Forest Dwellers (Recognition of Rights) Act 2006 to get 'community ownership' of their forest lands in 2012.

15 Savyasaachi, *Tribal Forest Dwellers and Self Rule: The Constituent Assembly Debates in India* (New Delhi, Indian Social Institute, 1998).

16 Archana Prasad, *Adivasis and the Trajectories of Political Mobilization in Contemporary India* in Meena Radhakrishna (ed.), *First Citizens: Studies on Adivasis, Tribals, and Indigenous Peoples in India* (Delhi, Oxford University Press, 2016).

17 Felix Padel and Samarendra Das, *Out of this Earth: Adivasis and the Aluminium Cartel* (Hyderabad, Orient Blackswan, 2010).

1 8 For this point see Archana Prasad, *Against Ecological Romanticism* and Archana Prasad, 'Adivasis and the Trajectories of Political Mobilisation'.

19 Susana Devalle, *Discourses of Ethnicity: Culture and Protest in Jharkhand* (Delhi, Sage Publications, 1992).

20 For example, see Archana Prasad, *Red Flag of the Warlis: History of an Ongoing Struggle* (Leftword Books, 2017).

21 Dasaratha Debbarma, *Ganamukti Parishad in Building the Peasant Movement in Tripura* (All India Kisan Sabha, Golden Jubilee Publication, 1986) and E.M.S. Namboodripad, *The National Question in Kerala* (Bombay, Peoples Publishing House, 1952).

22 For an elaboration of this, see Archana Prasad, *Environmentalism and the Left*.

23 Archana Prasad, *Red Flag of the Warlis*.

24 For a discussion of both of these see Archana Prasad, 'Adivasis and the Trajectories of Political Mobilisation'.

25 These characteristics have been discussed in more detail in Archana Prasad, 'Class, Community and Identity: Politics of the Adivasi in Contemporary India' in Amiya Bagchi and Amita Chatterji (eds), *Marxism: With and Beyond Marx* (London, Routledge, 2015).

26 For instance, see Luisa Steur, 'Adivasis, Communists, and the Rise of Indigenism in Kerala', *Dialectical Anthropology*, 2011.

27 For elaboration of this, see Archana Prasad, 'RSS-Corporate Interface in Adivasi India', Peoples Democracy, 22 January 2017.

28 For a full account of this process, see Angana Chatterji, *Violent Gods: Hindu Nationalism in India's Present, Narratives from Orissa* (Delhi, Three Essays Collective, 2009).

29 For example, see, Udayon Misra, 'Victory for identity politics, not Hindutva in Assam' in *Economic and Political Weekly,* 51(22), 20–23, 2016.

30 Archana Prasad, 'Neoliberalism, Tribal Survival and Agrarian Distress'. The latest figures for diversion of forest lands in 2018 have been taken from www.indiastat.com accessed on 8 June 2020.

31 The latest employment data by social group is available on NSSO, *Annual Periodic Labour Force Survey, 2017-18* (Delhi, NSSO, 2019).

32 Archana Prasad, 'Conservation and Tribal Development in the Forest Rights Act: Looking Beyond the Joint Parliamentary Committee Report', Social Scientist, August 2006.

33 This is based on my unpublished calculations from Annual Periodic Labour Force Survey, 2017-2018, National Sample Survey Organisation.

34 Archana Prasad, 'Adivasis and the Trajectories of Political Mobilisation'.

35 Archana Prasad, 'Adivasis and the Anatomy of a Conflict Zone: Bastar 2016', *Economic and Political Weekly*, June 2016.

Lessons from the Institution of 'Indigenous Self-Governance'

1 According to the Ho tribe, the system of self-governance is called 'Pir' or 'Manki Pir' and the head of the governance system is also called 'Manki Pir'.

2 Kolhan region in Jharkhand comprises West Singhbhum, East Singhbhum and Saraikela Kharsawan districts. This region is largely populated by Ho and Munda tribes. The self-governance system of Hos is called Pir or Manki Pir and the head of the Manki Pir is called Manki or Manki-Munda or Munda-Manki.

3 'Munda' is also the name of a tribe which resides in Khunti, Bundu, Tamar, Chaibasa and other areas of Jharkhand.

4 'Settle wastes' here means unused land. The unused land in the village in Kolhan region is given by the Munda or Manki to any landless person. This right is not given to Parha Raja of Kurux or Doklo Sohor of Kharia tribe. Thus no one in the Kolhan region remains landless.

5 According to history, the British regime entered Chotanagpur region in 1765 by defeating joint forces of Nawabs of Oudh and Bengal. The British entered into agreement with the local kings to collect rent on their behalf. Local people were against paying rent to the

British government, hence there were repeated rebellions against the high rent and usurpation of their lands by outsiders. The then British Agent for Kolhan region, Sir Thomas Wilkinson decided to occupy the area by force. Finally, in 1837 Wilkinson decided that Kolhan be declared a 'Kolhan Separate Estate' with its head office in Chaibasa. He came out with what is called Wilkinson's Rule that says 'the traditional customary laws of Munda-Manki would continue to be followed'. This provision of Wilkinson continued even after the Independence of India. (https://indianexpress.com/article/india/in-jharkhand-village-a-secession-fancy-a-crackdown-5000412/) Tribals residing in Kolhan region claim the continuation of Wilkinson's Rule according to Article 372 (1) and (2) of the Indian Constitution which says, '. . . All the laws in force in the territory of India immediately before the commencement of this Constitution shall continue in force therein until altered or repealed or amended by a competent Legislature or other competent authority', which has not been done till date.

6   The terms 'Ho Mundas' and 'Ho Mankis' refer to the position of Munda and Manki of the Ho tribe. The Ho Mundas are responsible for civil issues at the village level, while Ho Mankis look after cluster-level criminal issues.

References

1.   Alpa Shah, 'The Dark Side of Indigeneity?: Indigenous People, Rights and Development in India'. *History Compass*, September 2007, 5(6):1806–1832.
      https://www.researchgate.net/publication/351272946_Doing_Things_Differently_Using_the_ABCD_Method_to_Negotiate_with_Local_Leaders_in_Community_Engagement_Projects/references, accessed on 5 January 2020.

2.   J.L. McKnight, J.P. Kretzmann, *Building Communities from the Inside Out: A Path Toward Finding and Mobilizing a Community's Assets* (Chicago, ACTA Publications, 1993).

3.   Kennedy C. Chinyowa, Mziwoxolo Sirayi and Selloane Mokuku, 'Doing Things Differently: Using the ABCD Method to Negotiate

with Local Leaders in Community Engagement Projects' *Journal of International Education and Leadership*, 2016, Volume 6 Issue 1 Spring.

4. Nandini Sundar, '"Custom" and "Democracy" in Jharkhand', *Economic and Political Weekly*, 8-14 October 2005, vol. 40, No. 41, pp. 4430-4434.

5. Nelson Maldonado-Torres (ed.), *Decoloniality at Large: Towards a Trans-Americas and Global Transmodern Paradigm (Introduction to Second Special Issue of 'Thinking through the Decolonial Turn')*, 2012. *TRANSMODERNITY*: Journal of Peripheral Cultural Production of the Luso-Hispanic World, 1(3). Permalink: https://escholarship. org/uc/item/58c9c4wh, accessed on Nov. 15, 2019.

6. Prashant Pandey, 'In Jharkhand village, a secession fancy and a crackdown'. https://indianexpress.com/article/india/in-jharkhand-village-a-secession-fancy-a-crackdown-5000412/ (2017). Accessed on 5 December 2020

7. Vincent Ekka, *Exploring Development through Indigenous Perspectives: A study of Kurux (Oraon) Community of Central India* (Unpublished Ph. D. thesis, 2017).

8. Virginius Xaxa, *State, Society and Tribes: Issues in Post-Colonial India*, (Noida, Dorling Kindersley Pvt. Ltd., 2008).

Silent Voices, Distant Dreams: India's Denotified Tribes

1 Thomas Perry, Company Magistrate, came to Etawah in the year 1811. It was under his administration that perhaps the first confirmation of thuggee was received. (Dash, 2005: 27–28).

2 Mike Dash, *Thug: The True Story of India's Murderous Cult* (London, Granta, 2006).

Captain William Sleeman and Captain Meadows Taylor, one a political officer and the other an administrator, almost contemporaries, are some of the principal figures in etching the canvas of the Thugee. Captain William Sleeman, born in 1788, is synonymous with the Thugee campaign. He more or less led it and announced its ending as well. Philip Meadows Taylor came to India in 1824 and charted an illustrious career as an able administrator in Nizam's territory.

3   J. Sleeman, *Thug, or A Million Murders* (London, Sampson Low, Marston & Co., 1933).

4   David Arnold, *Police Power and Colonial Rule: Madras 1859-1947* (Delhi, Oxford University Press, 1986).

5   Stewart Gordon, 'Scarf and Sword: Thugs, Marauders, and State-Formation in 18th Century Malwa', *Indian Economic and Social History Review*, 1969, 4.4, pp. 403–429.

6   P. Roy (1996), 'Discovering India, Imagining Thuggee', *Yale Journal of Criticism*, 1996, Yale, pp. 121–145.

7   Henry Schwarz, Wiley-Blackwell, *Constructing the Criminal Tribe in Colonia India: Acting Like a Thief*, 2010.

8   Mike Dash, *Thug: The True Story of India's Murderous Cult* (London, Granta, 2006); Ibid.

9   James Clifford, *The Predicament of Culture: Twentieth Century Ethnography, Literature, and Art* (Cambridge, Harvard University Press, 1988), p. 268.

10 A. Gramsci, Q. Hoare and G. Smith (eds. and trans.), *Selection from Prison Notebooks*, (Hyderabad. Orient Longman, 1996), p. 333.

11 TAG Report, 2006.

12 A. Dandekar, A. Mukhopadhyaya, S. Panda and N. Kulkarni, *DNT Survey I* (Unpublished, Social Science Centre, 1999).

13 A. Dandekar and M. Shrinivasan, *The NEG Intervention in the Areas of Denotified and Nomadic Tribes of Maharashtra: An Assessment* (New Delhi, New Education Group, 2008).

14 A.A. Ayyangar et al., *The Criminal Tribes Act Enquiry Committee* (Govt of India, 1951), p. 3.

15 Ibid., p. 104.

16 A. Dandekar, A. Mukhopadhyaya, S. Panda and N. Kulkarni, *DNT Survey I* (Unpublished, Social Science Centre, 1999).

References

David Arnold, *Police Power and Colonial Rule: Madras 1859-1947* (Delhi, Oxford University Press, 1986).

James Clifford, *The Predicament of Culture: Twentieth Century Ethnography, Literature, and Art* (Cambridge, Harvard University Press, 1988).

Mike Dash, *Thug: The True Story of India's Murderous Cult* (London, Granta, 2006).

A. Dandekar, A. Mukhopadhyaya, S. Panda and N. Kulkarni, *DNT Survey I* (Unpublished, Social Science Centre, 1999).

A. Dandekar and M. Shrinivasan, *The NEG Intervention in the Areas of Denotified and Nomadic Tribes of Maharashtra: An Assessment* (New Delhi, New Education Group, 2008).

G.N. Devy, Rudolf Heredia, Ajay Dandekar, Meena Radhakrishnan, Anil Pandey, Kanji Patel, K.M. Metry and M. Aslam, *Waiting for Freedom. Report of the Technical Advisory Group on Denotified, Nomadic and Semi nomadic Tribes, The TAG Report* (New Delhi, Govt of India, 2006).

H.A. Giroux, *Ideology, Agency and the Process of Schooling*, Ed L. Barton and S. Walker (eds.), *Social Crisis and Educational Research* (London, Croom Helms, 1981).

Stewart Gordon, 'Scarf and Sword: Thugs, Marauders, and State-Formation in 18th Century Malwa', *Indian Economic and Social History Review,* 1969, 4.4, pp. 403–429.

A. Gramsci, Q. Hoare and G. Smith (eds. and trans.), *Selection from Prison Notebooks*, (Hyderabad, Orient Longman, 1996).

H. Gupta, 'A Critical Study of the Thugs and Their Activities', *Journal of Indian History,* August 1959, XXXVII, Part II, Serial No. 110, pp. 169–177.

NAC Working Group Report, https://nomadsgroup.files.wordpress.com/2010/04/dnt_draft.pdf

A.A. Ayyangar et al, *The Criminal Tribes Act Enquiry Committee* (Govt of India, 1951).

P. Roy (1996), 'Discovering India, Imagining Thuggee', *Yale Journal of Criticism*, 1996, Yale, pp. 121–145.

J. Sleeman, *Thug, or A Million Murders* (London, Sampson Low, Marston & Co., 1933).

Philip Meadows Taylor, (2002) *Confessions of a Thug* (New Delhi, Rupa, 2002).

Speak Up a Revolution

1   James Painter (ed.), interview with the author in *India's Media Boom: The Good News and the Bad* (Reuters Institute for the Study

of Journalism, Department of Politics and International Relations, University of Oxford, 2013).

Indigenous Republic (Indigenocracy)

1   'Report of the Indian Irrigation Commission, 1901–03', *Government Central Printing Office, Simla, Government of India*, 1903, https://indianculture.gov.in/report-indian-irrigation-commission-1901-03-0

How Not to Manage 'Tribal Affairs'

1   These claims are based on media reports mainly of early 2018.
2   The UPA government had constituted a National Advisory Council (NAC) for providing advice to the government on social policy matters.

On advice from the NAC, the Ministry of Tribal Affairs appointed a committee to prepare a 'Tribal Status Report'. The committee was headed by Prof Virginius Xaxa, who is among the contributors to this volume. The report came to be known as the Xaxa Committee Report, submitted in 2014.
3   The RSS provides funding and administrative support to the ABVP. Social activists working in tribal areas often become targets of RSS-affiliated organizations. They are now called 'urban Naxals'. Many of them are imprisoned.

The Life and Legacy of Abhay Xaxa

1   First published in *The India Forum*, 3 April 2020, *https://www.theindiaforum.in/article/memoriam-sociologist-activist-abhay-xaxa*
2   'If our Poop Protest is considered uncivil, then tell me what is Civil in this country', *India Resists*, 20 March 2015, https://www.indiaresists.com/if-our-poop-protest-is-considered-uncivil-then-tell-me-what-is-civil-in-this-country/
3   https://twitter.com/AdivasisMatter/status/1163821693678182400
4   Beena J. Pallical and N. Paul Divakar, 'Remembering Abhay Xaxa, the activist whose focus on emancipating Adivasi lives was second

to none', Firstpost, 23 March 2020, https://www.firstpost.com/
living/remembering-abhay-xaxa-the-activist-whose-focus-on-
emancipating-adivasi-lives-was-second-to-none-8176571.html

5   Kritika Sharma, 'Nearly 57% of India's teaching faculty belong to
general category, STs least represented', ThePrint.in, 27 July 2018,
https://theprint.in/india/governance/57-of-indias-teaching-faculty-
belong-to-general-category-sts-least-represented/89546/

6   '"It's a long fight against the old structures of caste, dominance and
inequality" - Abhay Xaxa', *Sabrang*, 15 February 2019, https://
sabrangindia.in/interview/its-long-fight-against-old-structures-
caste-dominance-and-inequality-abhay-xaxa

7   Maroona Murmu, 'Structural Violence of Casteism: A Personal
Narrative by an Adivasi University Teacher', *The India Forum*, 4
October 2019, https://www.theindiaforum.in/article/structural-
violence-casteism

About the Contributors

Naresh Chandra Saxena is the topper of the 1964 batch of the Indian Administrative Services. He retired as Secretary, Planning Commission, in 2002. He worked as Secretary in the Ministry of Rural Development from 1997–1999. From 1993 to 996, he served as the director of the Lal Bahadur Shastri National Academy of Administration in Mussoorie. Saxena was awarded his doctorate in forestry from University of Oxford in 1992. He was awarded an honorary PhD from the University of East Anglia in the UK in 2006. He recently wrote a book, *What Ails the IAS and Why It Fails to Deliver: An Insider's View.*

Virginius Xaxa was earlier a professor of sociology at Delhi School of Economics, the Guwahati campus of Tata Institute of Social Sciences and Tezpur University. Presently, he is a visiting professor at Institute for Human Development in New Delhi.

Meenakshi Natarajan works for the cause of empowerment of the citizenry. She is currently a part of the Rajiv Gandhi Panchayati Raj Sangathan of the Indian National Congress. The sangathan is dedicated towards the devolution of power and gram swaraj, and organizes Sarvoday Sankalp Shivirs in every district. Natarajan has travelled to all tribal districts and blocks in India, and has worked towards spreading awareness about the Panchayats (Extension to the Scheduled Areas) Act (PESA), the Forest Rights Act (FRA) and Gram Sabhas. A former Lok Sabha MP and president of the National Students' Union of India (NSUI), she also led the Youth Congress in Madhya Pradesh. Natarajan has authored a book, titled *1857 Bhartiya Paripekshay,* and a novel, titled *Apne Apne Kurukshetra.* She is the recipient of the Vageshwari Samman and the Pakhi Shabd Sadhak Samman for her novel.

Kantilal Bhuria is an MLA from Jhabua Assembly constituency. He has represented the constituency five times in the past as MLA. A five-time MP from Jhabua, Bhuria served as the Union Minister of State for Agriculture, Food and Civil Supplies, and as the Union Minister of Tribal Affairs. He played a significant role in drafting and enacting the Forest Rights Act, 2006, which gave tribals across India land-holding rights. Bhuria is also the former state president of the Indian National Congress in Madhya Pradesh.

Vikrant Bhuria is a gold medalist in general surgery from Mahatma Gandhi Memorial Medical College, Indore. Bhuria is dedicated to the cause and ideology of all-inclusive development of his countrymen. At present, he is the state president of the Indian Youth Congress in Madhya Pradesh. He has served as the president of the Junior Doctors' Association in Madhya Pradesh. Bhuria works for tribal rights and better medical facilities for them. He is the recipient of the Ambedkar Ratna for social service in tribal areas. He was conferred the award by the former Supreme Court Chief Justice, Justice K.G. Balakrishnan.

Archana Prasad is a professor at the Centre for Informal Sector and Labour Studies at Jawaharlal Nehru University in New Delhi. Some of her recent books include *Against Ecological Romanticism: Verrier Elwin and the Making of an Anti-Modern Tribal Identity* (2003), *Environmentalism and the Left: Contemporary Debates and Future*

Agendas (2004) and *The Red Flag of the Warlis: History of an Ongoing Struggle* (2017), which was translated in Marathi in 2020 and in Hindi in 2021.

Vincent Ekka currently heads the Department of Tribal Studies at the Indian Social Institute in New Delhi. He has a doctorate in sociology from Jawaharlal Nehru University in New Delhi. Ekka is currently engaged in social research on indigenous issues in central and north India. Indigenous issues, self-governance, indigenous perspectives and indigeneity are some of his interest areas for research and study.

Ajay Dandekar conducts research into pastoralism and pastoral nomadic groups of the Deccan in their historical settings. His research areas also encompass issues related to the agrarian crisis, tribal governance and Denotified Tribes. He is a faculty member in the Department of History at Shiv Nadar University.

S. Choudhary is an International Center for Journalists (ICFJ) Knight Fellow. He is the founder of CGNet Swara, a platform to discuss Adivasi issues in the tribal belt of central India, particularly related to Gondwana. Choudhary was a TV and radio producer for BBC's South Asia bureau for eight years and a reporter for the *Guardian*'s South Asia bureau for two years. He also served as a media trainer for the BBC World Service Trust, the United Nations and various Indian universities. He produced the first television coverage of foreign militants operating in Kashmir and conducted the first television interview with the chief commander of a Kashmiri militant organization. He was a reporter for five years with *Deshbandhu*, a Hindi daily.

Ghanshyam was born in a small Adivasi village, Mahuadabar, in Deoghar district in Jharkhand. He participated in the Jayaprakash Narayan movement for total revolution and was actively involved in the Jharkhand andolan. He has composed and published several books, including his most famous work, *Indigenocracy*. He was conferred the Jayaprakash Narayan Youth Award by Baba Amte. Ghanshyam has received several awards and recognition for his social work in Jharkhand and Bihar.

Chitrangada Choudhury is an independent multimedia journalist and associate professor at Krea University. She serves on the editorial board of Article 14, a website dedicated to issues of justice, democracy and the Indian Constitution. Her work focuses on rural issues, in particular indigenous communities, and issues of environmental and social justice. Her reportage has been cited for multiple awards, including Sanskriti Journalism Award, Press Council of India's National Awards for Excellence in Journalism in the category of investigative reporting and the Lorenzo Natali Media Prize. Choudhury's research has appeared in peer-reviewed journals and anthologies. She co-authored a study on the Panchayats (Extension to the Scheduled Areas) Act (PESA) for the State of Panchayati Raj Report in 2010 for the Union Ministry of Panchayati Raj.

Aniket Aga teaches environmental studies and anthropology at Krea University. He is interested in science and technology studies, democratic politics and agrarian studies, with a focus on environmental justice and sustainable agriculture. He is the author of *Genetically Modified Democracy: Transgenic Crops in Contemporary India,* which was published in 2021.

About Samruddha Bharat Foundation

Samruddha Bharat Foundation is an independent sociopolitical organization established after the Dr B.R. Ambedkar International Conference held in July 2017 to:

1. Further India's constitutional promise
2. Forge an alliance of progressive forces
3. Encourage a transformative spirit in Indian politics and society.

Addressing both the symbolic and the substantive, SBF works to shape the polity, serve as a platform for participatory democracy, shape public discourse and deepen engagement with the diaspora.

In doing so, SBF works closely with India's major secular political parties on normative and policy issues. It has also created a praxis between India's foremost academics, activists and policymakers, as well as people's movements, civil society organizations, think tanks and institutions. Finally, it has established Bridge India as a sister organization in the United Kingdom to do similar work with the diaspora.

For further details, see:

www.samruddhabharat.in

@SBFIndia

Samruddha Bharat Foundation

@SBFIndia